IMAGE

THE HISTORIC TOWN
OF PICTOU

MONICA GRAHAM

NIMBUS
PUBLISHING

Acknowledgements

This book would not have been possible to write without The Pictou Historical Photograph Society: Bill Sinclair, Bruce G. Murray, Amy Murray, Beth Henderson, Eric LeBlanc, Don MacIsaac, and Raymond (Labman) Gregory. This group collected many of the photos included here for a 2003 exposition entitled The Way We Were, and gave me permission to use them in this book.

Don, Beth, Eric, Bill, and Ray also allowed me to consult them for valuable information and insight about Pictou's past, and shared anecdotes that made the past come alive.

Don MacIsaac has not only collected several boxes of historic photos over the years, but has personally photographed Pictou milestones and landmarks since the 1930s, and has kept careful records of his subjects.

Pictou Mayor Lawrence LeBlanc provided meticulously documented photos, and allowed me access to his considerable library of obscure Pictou-related publications. Dolly Battist, Alfie Dalton, Gertrude Holton, and Henry Snow shared old newspaper clipping, photos, and information. Jim Nicholson, Janet Johnston, Marianne MacMillan, Cathe Maclean, and Barbara Kittilsen graciously answered my last-minute queries for information.

Special thanks to my husband, Martin, for his technical help and patience.

To all of you, thank you.

— Monica Graham

Copyright © Monica Graham, 2004

All rights reserved. No part of this book may be reproduced, stored in a retrieval system, or transmitted in any form or by any means without the prior written permission from the publisher, or, in the case of photocopying or other reprographic copying, permission from Access Copyright, 1 Yonge Street, Suite 1900, Toronto, Ontario M5E 1E5.

Nimbus Publishing Limited
PO Box 9166, Halifax, NS B3K 5M8
(902) 455-4286

Printed and bound in Canada
Design: Terri Strickland

Front cover: County courthouse, 1899, see page 10
Title page: Front Street, Looking West, 1912, see page 17

Library and Archives Canada Cataloguing in Publication

> Graham, Monica, 1954-
> The historic town of Pictou :
> images of our past / Monica Graham.
> Includes bibliographical references.
> ISBN 1-55109-501-7
>
> 1. Pictou (N.S.)—History—Pictorial works. I. Title.
> FC2349.P5G72 2004   971.6'13   C2004-905517-8

Canadä   The Canada Council | Le Conseil des Arts
         for the Arts | du Canada

We acknowledge the financial support of the Government of Canada through the Book Publishing Industry Development Program (BPIDP) and the Canada Council for our publishing activities.

Contents

Introduction iv

Chapter 1
    A Tour of the Town 1

Chapter 2
    A Place for People 29

Chapter 3
    Churches, Schools, and Hospitals 53

Chapter 4
    Transportation 75

Chapter 5
    To Arms 95

Chapter 6
    The Town at Work 105

Chapter 7
    Pictou Pleasures 125

Conclusion 136

Bibliography 137

Photo credits 137

Introduction

The historic seaport of Pictou, on Nova Scotia's northern shore, owes its existence to geography. Its south-facing location, on the north side of a sheltered harbour near Gulf of St. Lawrence transportation routes, has attracted settlers and commerce for centuries.
The wealth of land and sea first attracted humans to the area more than 10,000 years ago.

The first Europeans to visit the harbour found the dense forest already inhabited by Mi'kmaq, who won their food, shelter, and clothing from what, at first, appeared to be a wild and inhospitable country.

Shellfish, game animals, and birds were plentiful, huge trees grew tall and wide, and the saltmarsh estuaries of the East, Middle, and West rivers, and safe beaches at the harbour mouth, offered ample village sites. This bounty could not be kept secret forever.

Some historians believe the Orkney Islands' Prince Henry Sinclair was the first European to arrive at Pictou Harbour. They cite his expedition reports from 1398, which tell of visiting with the friendly Mi'kmaq and of flame and smoke spewing from an exposed coal seam, upstream from a safe harbour.

In 1672 the French explorer Nicolas Denys sailed up Pictou Harbour as far as his boat would take him, and wrote a glowing report of the of native people and their land. He and the Acadians, who settled along the Northumberland shore outside the harbour, traded with the Mi'kmaq for fish and furs. The Acadians left when their compatriots up the coast, in present-day Colchester and Cumberland counties and New Brunswick, were rounded up by the British and deported.

As far as British land speculators were concerned, the expulsion left the land vacant for new English settlers. Occupation by the native people counted little, because they were more inclined to share resources than lay individual claim to them; and because the Europeans considered themselves superior. Thus, the empty land was opened to settlers.

The ship *Hector*'s Scottish passengers, who arrived on September 15, 1773, are credited with creating Pictou as the "Birthplace of New Scotland," but they weren't the town's founders. Six years earlier, on June 10, 1767, the ship *Betsey* arrived from Philadelphia with 35 Scottish-Irish settlers, two Black slaves, and a convict working off his sentence, all led by the Harris and Patterson families. They were met by Truro citizens who trudged about sixty miles over the hills to welcome them.

Both the *Betsey* and the *Hector* settlers were there courtesy of a rush to settle

ENTRANCE TO PICTOU HARBOUR FROM THE GOLF LINKS, C.1905

1760–1770s land grants before they expired. Land elsewhere in Nova Scotia was snapped up, but Pictou Harbour and other north shore grants, being more distant from the centres in New England, were unfamiliar and undeveloped.

Merchants in Boston, New York, and London dreamed of acquiring huge tracts of land and re-selling them to make a quick bundle of money. One of them was Alexander McNutt, Nova Scotia's agent in Boston, who claimed George II had made him an honorary colonel. He was associated with all sixteen land companies bidding for Nova Scotia land in 1765, including the Philadelphia Company. More than two million acres were handed out in one two-week period that year, and more than half went to McNutt and his associates.

The grants were conditional on settling a stipulated number of people on the land within a certain time period. Despite getting the choicest grants and conditions, McNutt was unable to comply, and was forced to give up his grant at Pictou harbour, called the Irish grant, in 1769.

When McNutt's associates in the Philadelphia Company made a serious

HECTOR PIONEER MONUMENT ON MARKET SQUARE, DESIGNED BY NEW GLASGOW SCULPTOR JOHN WILSON AND DONATED BY THE ST. ANDREW'S SOCIETY IN 1923.

effort to settle their 200,000-acre grant in 1765, they found that it included no harbour access because McNutt held all that land, and John Fisher held the water frontage across the harbour, in what is now Pictou Landing. The boundaries were re-drawn after the Philadelphia Company complained to the government, but, even then, its harbour frontage was mostly swamp and alders near the mouth of the West River.

In 1766, the company persuaded six families to emigrate from New England to Pictou aboard the *Betsey*. After putting them and their provisions ashore, the *Betsey* sailed away in the middle of the night before the settlers could change their minds. "Picture the loneliness of that little band," wrote Pictou historian Rev. George Patterson in 1877. The land was not cleared as they had expected, and "their hearts sank."

One *Betsey* family left, but the rest stayed and were joined the following year by two families from Truro and two from Pennsylvania, followed in 1769 by sixty-seven more— and a few others departed the colony. By the end of 1769 there were 120 inhabitants remaining at what was called Donegal Township, but no more interest in moving to Pictou could be generated among New Englanders. The Philadelphia Company principals concluded that the venture was not a moneymaker. Then, in 1772, the Philadelphia Company's Dr. John Witherspoon contacted a business partner in Scotland, John Pagan, to seek settlers on the other side of the Atlantic.

The time was ripe. Scottish citizens needed a change. Their bid for freedom from the English had failed in the horror and bloodshed on Culloden Moor, on April 16, 1746, when an army of nine thousand led by the Duke of Cumberland, Prince William, defeated

Prince Charles Edward Stuart's Highlanders.

To curb insurrection after Culloden, the English burned the Highlanders' homes and their crops, executed suspected rebels or shipped them to the colonies as prison labour, and slaughtered their cattle. The English then banned both the highland plaid and the bagpipes, calling the latter weapons of war. Next, the English cancelled the seven-hundred-year-old hereditary clan system and seized the chieftains' lands, whether or not they had rebelled against the English Crown.

The English replaced the feudal system with a tenancy commission to lease land to farmers, but rents skyrocketed and farm production fell. By 1768, whole communities of economically beleaguered Scots quit, and sailed for a new start in places like the Carolinas, Virginia, and St. John Island (Prince Edward Island).

Enter the *Hector:* a battered Dutch smuggling brig, already old when John Pagan bought it in the 1760s. Pagan advertised that the *Hector* would sail for Pictou by May 15, 1773, promising through his agent John Ross that each settler would get passage, between two hundred and one thousand acres, a year's food supply at cost, and accommodation until they could build their own homes.

The initial response was so small that the ship didn't leave Ullapool, in Loch Broom, until early July. It carried a motley collection of 189 Highlanders whose surnames—and descendants—are still found in Pictou's telephone book. There were MacKenzies, Sutherlands, Grants, and Frasers; Catholics and Protestants; a jailbird and a laird's son; a widow and more than seventy children; and farmers and bankers. One, a MacKay, didn't have the money for his fare, but Captain John Speirs let him aboard when the other passengers agreed to share their food with him, because his bagpipe playing would lift their spirits.

The weather was fine when the *Hector* left port, but it turned worse out on the Atlantic. So did the Highlanders' health—first with seasickness, and then dysentery and smallpox. Eighteen passengers died, mostly children.

Off Newfoundland in August, a gale struck and set the voyage back by two weeks, which meant the passengers had to eke out their food and water supply. Tired, sick, and hungry, they arrived at Pictou on September 15, 1773, too late to plant crops that season, but in time to face their first Canadian winter.

The land was forested in a way the Highlanders had never dreamed possible. There was

THE LAUNCHING OF THE *HECTOR* REPLICA, SEPTEMBER 17, 2000

THE OLD COLLEGE, C.1920

nowhere to live, and most had no idea how to build a log house—or even use a felling axe. Land surveyed for them by Robert Patterson, who had laid out the *Betsey* settlers' lots, was miles away in the hills. It might as well have been on the moon, as the Highlanders feared both the wild animals and the Mi'kmaq—who had fled to the woods in fear when they heard MacKay play the pipes.

The *Betsey* people tried to help the newcomers, but they had little enough themselves. There was also a language gap—most of the *Hector* settlers spoke Gaelic, not English—which created some conflict with the Americans, as the *Betsey* settlers were called.

When the ship *Hector* returned to the harbour that fall, the captain refused the settlers their supplies because they had not taken up their grants, so the Highlanders took what they needed, kept careful account, and paid later. Like the *Betsey* people before them, they somehow made it through their first winter. Most walked to Truro or Windsor to work as labourers, but about seventy stayed at the harbour, barely surviving on their meagre supplies and what they could hunt or gather.

In the spring of 1774, many of the *Hector* people who had gone to Truro returned to Pictou, and they began moving up the rivers to settle the land allotted to them. In 1776, the same year more Scottish settlers arrived to share their meagre resources, the American Revolution brought still another hardship on the tiny community. Until then, Pictou had been supplied with British goods through the Thirteen Colonies, but that trade stopped with American independence. The flow of supplies resumed when John Patterson initiated direct trade with Scotland in 1779, the beginning of Pictou's lucrative shipping industry.

The American Revolution divided the community, with the Scots sympathizing with the British, and the *Betsey* settlers supporting the Americans. Friends suspected each other of spying, and residents had to take an oath of allegiance—which some refused to do. An American privateer's capture of a cargo vessel off Merigomish created some concern in Pictou that the town was about to be attacked. Residents grabbed their muskets and ran to Battery Hill, overlooking the harbour, but the attack didn't happen.

In 1777, American sympathizers in Pictou seized Captain Thomas Lowden and his ship, loading timber in the harbour for the British market. The captors abandoned the boat up the coast, where Lowden recovered it. The incident made Pictou too hot for the American settlers, and many left without selling their property. Other American privateers—pirates sanctioned by their government—cruised the Northumberland shore, but Pictou had little worth stealing, so wasn't bothered.

The settlers owned little more than what they stood up in, but the Mi'kmaq taught them to hunt, build canoes and use snowshoes, and accepted rent for the use of their corn patches, the only cultivated land. The natives' friendliness was a bonus, because just a few years before the *Betsey's* arrival, the Pictou Mi'kmaq, or Pectougwak, had agreed with the British that they would cease their raids on white settlements in return for exclusive use of their ancestral lands along the Northumberland Strait. The subsequent arrival of settlers caused some resentment among the Mi'kmaq, and even the friendly natives occasionally became impatient with the newcomers' ways. Two men, Patlass and Lulan, were well-known and popular figures in the Pictou settlement around 1800, and others sold baskets and other items in the town.

But disease and alcohol, coupled with the destruction of game habitat by increased farming, led to a decline in the Mi'kmaw population that threatened to eliminate them altogether. The Mi'kmaq retreated to a reservation at Pictou Landing, and survived. The settlers survived too, but it was a struggle for both. Years of bad crops, rodents, and cold summers, and backbreaking work dogged the pioneers, who were joined by boatload after boatload of new immigrants fleeing hardship in Scotland.

They spread inland to the valleys and hills, founding thriving villages that grew into New Glasgow, Westville, Trenton, and Stellarton; or that dwindled into little more than a few homes and fields and a name on a map: Millsville, Gairloch, Glencoe, Auchencairn, or Lovat. One of the new arrivals was Rev. Dr. James MacGregor, a Presbyterian minister called from Scotland in 1786 by "Deacon" John Patterson of the harbour and leaders of the upriver communities. MacGregor arrived in Halifax on July 11, rode to Truro by horseback, and on to Pictou on July 21. He started work the next day, preaching in Squire Patterson's barn—in English in the morning, and in Gaelic in the afternoon.

MacGregor preached outdoors and in private homes from River John to Merigomish, travelling mostly by foot and canoe, as there were few horses. Away from home for weeks

SHIPS AT PICTOU DOCKS, C.1914

on end, he visited people of every denomination, as he was the only minister. He encouraged schools, and built the first two churches in the county, at New Glasgow and Loch Broom, in 1787, but he wasn't paid until 1788.

The civilizing effect of MacGregor's ministry attracted others to Pictou, where the former McNutt grant had changed hands a few times until Deacon John Patterson, one of the *Hector* people, bought it in 1787. He laid out building lots where the town centre now stands, and sold them on the condition that the buyer build on them, or pay a penalty. Patterson also built small homes to rent or sell, and the town's first, modest wharf.

In 1788 Thomas Copeland built Pictou's first ship, to be followed by hundreds over the years. The French Revolution, beginning in 1793, prompted a brisk trade in timber for shipbuilding. Pictou's tall, straight timbers and the fine harbour attracted more merchants and shipbuilders: Captain Lowden, who skidded logs down Deacon's Hill to the shore and also built the windmill where the Customs House now stands; Banffshire entrepreneur Edward Mortimer, who owned Pictou's first two-wheeled cart yet died penniless; John Pagan's merchant sons, Robert and Thomas; and Halifax merchant Hugh Denoon, later a judge and customs collector. These people settled in or near Patterson's town, but as land was taken up in the vicinity, others moved inland, or farther afield to Cape Breton and Prince Edward Island.

All the immigrants arrived through the only port of entry, Pictou, named after failed attempts to call it after the lost homelands of its founders. The community had variously been known as Coleraine, Donegal, New Paisley, Alexandria, Teignmouth, Southampton, and Walmsley. The map-makers finally decided on Pictou, derived from the Mi'kmaw *Agg Piktuk*, or explosive place, describing a burning coal seam near what is now Stellarton. The name applied to the whole region, today's Pictou County, as well as to the harbour town.

By 1792, Pictou had a jail, followed by court sessions in 1797, and then poll and property taxes. In 1799, the people voted for fish and timber merchant Edward Mortimer, a reformer, in the first election.

By 1803, lumbering was the most lucrative business in Pictou, with fifty vessels loading squared timber that year for Britain. Many farmers spent more time cutting, sawing, and rafting timber than they did planting crops, but the soil was so rich that farming prospered anyway. Dr. MacGregor, by then focusing his ministry in the New Glasgow–Stellarton area, complained about the prevalence of rum; a society was established to assist the natives (who did not necessarily want to be helped); and there was an outcry about the squalid conditions aboard the immigrant ships. The town consisted of less than twenty buildings, including barns, the jail, a tavern, and a smithy.

Into this situation arrived Rev. Dr. Thomas McCulloch, in the fall of 1803. He was headed for Prince Edward Island, but it was too late in the season to continue his journey, so he stayed in Pictou and temporarily ministered to the Harbour, as it was called. He held services in a shed at Windmill Hill, and later at the tavern. The next year, when it came time to move on to Prince Edward Island, he decided to stay in Pictou.

McCulloch's legacy includes First Church, built in 1804, and Pictou Academy, founded in 1816 to offer education to all, regardless of religious or political stripe, and to provide future candidates for the ministry. Although the Academy was never allowed to grant degrees as Dr. McCulloch wished, its graduates made their marks in Nova Scotia and elsewhere. The school, still in existence, has produced at least three hundred clergy and eight college presidents, including the prominent geologist Sir John William Dawson, first president of McGill University. Other notable graduates were World War Two commander of the Canadian Navy, Admiral Leonard Murray; the Frontier College founder, Alfred Fitzpatrick; the 1932 Canadian representative to the League of Nations, Henry Munro; A. H. MacKay, an Academy principal and Nova Scotia's superintendent of education from 1891 to 1926; and sisters Jemima and Mary MacKenzie, medical missionaries to India.

The initial Academy class produced Jotham Blanchard, who published the first newspaper outside Halifax, the *Colonial Patriot,* between 1827 and 1833. The lawyer used his newspaper to advocate reform, and successfully converted Joseph Howe, who later led the Nova Scotia struggle for responsible government.

McCulloch and MacGregor, along with other Presbyterian ministers who served Pictou in the early 1800s, were anti-burghers, opposed to the teachings of the established Church of Scotland. To their credit, they did not preach division to the congregations, who came from both branches of the church.

But when the church leaders met in 1817 to establish the Presbyterian Church of Nova Scotia, they scratched an itch that should have been left alone. Political lines of reform versus conservative deepened, following ecclesiastical divisions of secessionist versus establishment. New Scottish immigrants, arriving every week with their prejudices intact, demanded the same kind of teaching as they had left behind, regardless of what was tolerated in their new country. The conflict reached into every village, and divided families. Pictou Academy felt the split keenly. The school's trustees had difficulty obtaining funds because its secessionist theology was opposed by both the established Church of Scotland and the ruling Anglicans, who feared the new school's competition with their own Kings College.

In 1830, the so-called Brandy Election was fought over two issues—customs on liquor coming into Pictou and the debate over Pictou Academy. Both the Tories and the reformers brought in voters and enforcers. Arguments in the taverns led to street fighting, and days of violence. One man was killed, and the reformer (Liberal) Jotham Blanchard was elected.

In the end, the British government told the Nova Scotia government to fund the Academy, and the brandy tax was legislated. Dr. McCulloch, who had given up parochial work in order to devote his energies to the Academy, became principal of Dalhousie University in 1838, and died in 1843, thirteen years after Dr. MacGregor.

The episode gave Pictou a reputation as a hotbed of modern thought, augmented by the presence of a Literary and Scientific Society that encouraged the likes of the geologist J. William Dawson (later knighted and the president of McGill University) and chemist J. D. B. Fraser, the first to produce chloroform in Nova Scotia, in 1848.

While the church and state battled for hearts and souls, the population in Pictou grew, reaching fifteen hundred by 1830. A road between Pictou and Halifax was laid in 1792, and by 1828 the stagecoach fare was two pounds sterling, but the main highway was still the sea. John Foster ran a ferry across the harbour to Pictou Landing in 1807, and a canoe trip to New Glasgow was much less arduous than the overland route. In 1830, the steamboat *Richard Smith* began carrying coal from the upriver towns to Pictou for shipment abroad, and coal and iron from the inland communities soon replaced timber as the port's main export.

The ore was transported by horse, oxen, or—after the 1839 opening of Canada's first steam railroad from the East River to Abercrombie—by steel rail to docks at the mouths of the East, Middle, and West rivers. There the cargo was loaded onto barges and small boats to be shipped to bigger wharves at Pictou, where it was transferred to larger ships bound for Europe, up the St. Lawrence, and the American states.

So many vessels from all over the globe plied the harbour that at times ships had to wait for weeks to berth at the coal dock. It was said that in the mid-1800s one could cross the mile-wide harbour without ever wetting a foot, by stepping from one ship's deck to the next.

Nearly every trader had his own ship, or fleet of ships, and shipbuilding was a major industry in Pictou, as in other coastal communities. More shipping traffic led to more docking, shipbuilding, and repair facilities. Inns and taverns opened to serve sailors and travellers. The increasing demand for goods and services led to a healthy manufacturing and commercial sector, which, in turn, developed a need for churches, schools, hospitals, and entertainment to satisfy a growing population.

Pictou's importance as an east coast port, rivalled only by Montreal and Halifax, was established in history when the steamship *Royal William* sailed from the port in 1832 to cross the Atlantic, the first to do so under steam alone.

The town's economic stature led to Pictou County becoming separate from Halifax County in 1836, but it was not until December 1873 that Pictou was incorporated as a town. For a fee of forty-four dollars, Sheriff William H. Harris presided over the May 8 election, which saw lawyer David Matheson elected for a one-year term for an honorarium of four hundred dollars. It was harder to get a clerk. Two men refused the office before George H. Elliott, who later became mayor, accepted it with a salary of five hundred dollars a year. Council held its first meeting in the former county courthouse at George and Coleraine streets in June 1874.

AERIAL SHOT OF PICTOU, C.1920S

KEY

1. First Church
2. United Church
3. Pictou Academy
4. G.J. Hamilton & sons
5. Y.M.C.A.
6. Post Ofice
7. St. Andrew's Church
8. St. James Church
9. East End School
10. Stella Maris Church
11. Custom House
12. C.N. Station
13. C.N. Round House
14. C.N. Water Tower
15. Battery Hill

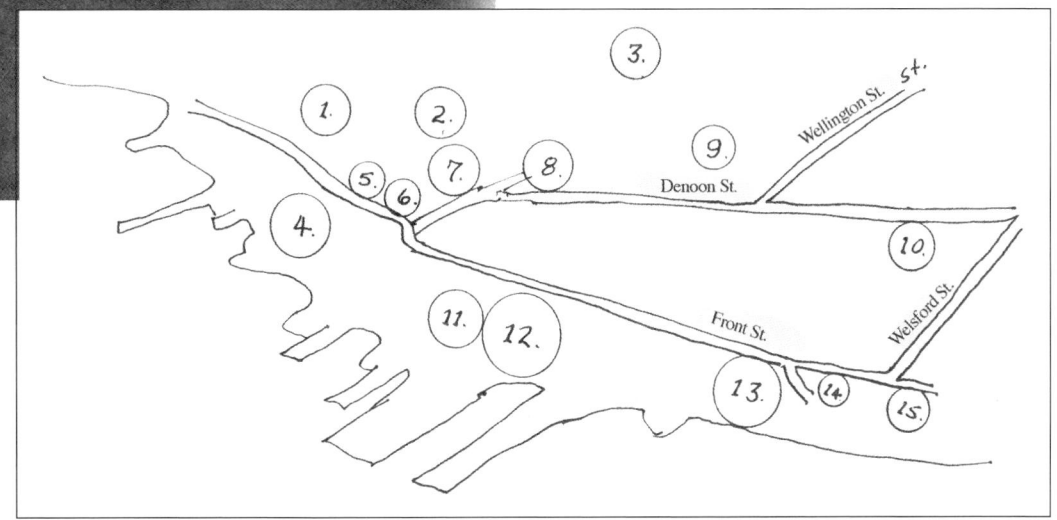

Introduction   xiii

PICTOU'S 1900 TOWN COUNCIL. BACK, FROM THE LEFT: MAGISTRATE CHARLES TANNER, TOWN CLERK FRED MACKARACHER, MAYOR A. J. CRAIG (SEATED), DAVID MACDONALD, JOHN D. MACDONALD. SEATED FROM LEFT: W. H. POPE, J. D. BAULIN, ADAM CARSON, J. SMITH GALLANT

Mayors of the Town of Pictou

David Matheson 1874
Charles Davis 1875, 1878
John McKinlay 1876–77
John MacLeod 1879–1883, 1886, 1906, 1909–10
Cornelius Dwyer 1884–85
George Elliott 1887–88
Allan Ferguson 1889–90
Howard Hamilton 1891–93
Daniel Sutherland 1894–96
James Yorston 1897–98
Alvin Craig 1899–1900
Alexander MacDonald 1901–05
J. Smith Grant 1907–08
James Primrose 1911–15
James Smith 1916–18

John Priest 1919–21, 1926–31
James Floyd 1922–23
John MacEachern 1924–25
Dr. M. R. Young 1932–1936
Thomas R. Hooper 1937–1940
John F MacDonald 1941
Thomas MacKay 1942–43
H. F. Harper 1944–47
Allan A. Ferguson 1948–57
J. H. Baillie 1957–61
Max Russell 1961–65
Clarence MacCarthy 1966–79
Ernie Jordan 1979–88
Dan Currie 1988–91
Lawrence LeBlanc 1991–

Chapter 1

A Tour of the Town

WESTWARD VIEW, 1905

This view of Faulkland Street shows the clock tower of Knox Presbyterian Church on the left, and the lower, four-spired square steeple of Prince Street Presbyterian in the middle. Norway Point is in the middle distance, and the Mile Bridge, between Brown's Point and Loch Broom, can be seen faintly. On the left is Abercrombie Point, which in 1968 became one end of the Pictou causeway. The cove slightly right of centre was said to be haunted by the ghosts of a Halifax press gang trying to kidnap Pictou men for Navy ships. In the eighteenth and early nineteenth centuries it was the practice of the British Navy to press, or force, male civilians into service aboard warships. Nine men were killed in the melee and buried on the shore of the cove. The ladder-like structures beside the street are protection for saplings that are today mature, well-leafed trees.

CHARRED LANDMARK, 1872

An early Pictou landmark, the Quebec Hotel on Coleraine Street burned in 1872. The home on the left of the photo, built by John MacKay in 1819, was spared the flames. John was the son of William MacKay, who had permission from Governor John Wentworth to mine the coal seam he found on his farm, about 20 miles inland near present-day Stellarton. John and his brother Alexander collected the coal in flat-bottomed boats and floated it down the river to sell to townspeople as fuel for their homes. John also used the coal to fuel his blacksmith shop, one of the first in Pictou. Eight years after settling on the corner, John put the house, shop, and land, which ran the length of Coleraine Street, on the market. The home has double walls, two cellars, and 13-inch windowsills. It was used by the Salvation Army from 1927 to 1952, and then as a gift shop and private home. The Prest family now owns it.

OLD MARKET, 1875

The octagonal market building with its round tower was once the busiest place in Pictou. Built in 1852 at Market Square, between Water and Church streets, it had shutters instead of glass windows and a six-foot-wide wooden platform around it. It closed in the winter, but in summer it was open from 8:00 A.M. until 6:00 P.M. It was fitted with indoor stalls and a meat-cutting room with butcher blocks and scales. Farmers and butchers, like James Marshall, William Pope, and Charles Meagher, rented a stall for ten dollars a year. Those who couldn't afford indoor space spread their wares on the grass outside.

Customers could get beef or pork for four cents a pound, butter for twelve cents a pound, a dozen eggs for ten cents, and two chickens for thirty cents. When the building was demolished in the 1920s, Sheriff Sim Harris took the round tower for use as a garden house. Bandmaster John Stramberg directed the construction of a bandstand in its place, and the Hector monument was placed uphill from it in 1923.

SHORELINE BY FRONT STREET, 1875

The cove on the right is now the site of the Ricky Sutherland Memorial ball field, next to the former railway station. The cove was filled in during the 1890s to make room for the railway station and roundhouse. Stella Maris Roman Catholic Church is on the horizon. The large white house in the centre of the photo is the Front Street home built by W. H. Davies. His company established the Pictou foundry in the early 1800s, and worked on the *Royal William* before it crossed the Atlantic in 1833. The oldest of the long, low, brick foundry buildings next door dates back to 1854. The company built stoves, engines, boilers, pumps, and mining machinery. Alan A. Ferguson bought it in 1906 and developed Pictou Foundry and Machine Company, and later bought the Pictou shipyard.

WATER STREET IN 1885

On the left at the end of Water Street on Coleraine Street is the store and home built by John A. Stalker, who also built and outfitted the Pictou Bank next door. The bank opened in 1874 with $500,000 capital, with John Crerar as president and Robert P. Grant of the Nova Scotia Assembly as vice-president. Other directors were New Glasgow Mayor Jeffrey McColl, Conservative Member of Parliament Robert Doull, and Pictou businessmen J. R. Noonan, William Gordon, and Isaac Grant. Thomas Watson, of Renfrew, Ontario, was the first manager. The bank had branches or agents in Montreal, Halifax, Amherst, Antigonish, Stellarton, New Glasgow, New York, and London (England). The Bank of British North America, a forerunner of the Royal Bank, had been in the town since 1830; the Bank of Nova Scotia was established in Pictou in 1839; a new government savings program paid four per cent interest; and the Pictou Mechanics Institute had a savings bank. By 1886, the Pictou Bank was in trouble and was taken over by the Bank of Nova Scotia, which eventually recovered its money, took over the Coleraine Street headquarters, and paid off shareholders, who had lost most of their investment. In 1909, the Bank of Nova Scotia finally closed the books on the Pictou Bank, one of twenty-six post-Confederation bank failures. Scotiabank still occupies the Pictou Bank's Coleraine Street premises.

FRONT STREET LOOKING EAST, 1890

This 1890 postcard of Front Street, looking towards Battery Hill, may have been purchased at James MacLean & Sons, shown on the left at the corner of Coleraine Street. The large store was established before 1879 to sell books, school supplies, stationery, wallpaper, postcards, souvenirs, and Canadian and foreign newspapers and magazines. The building was torn down in the 1970s, and the Bank of Nova Scotia, on the left but out of sight in this picture, expanded to the site. Prior to MacLean's occupying the corner, George Fogo operated a candy factory there. Across Front Street, on the right, was once James Mainland's grocery and liquor store.

THE SLIP ROAD, 1890

The slip road was an unofficial extension of Front Street, following the north side of Pictou Harbour seaward towards Yorston's slipway, where the shipyard is today. The slope at the right is the foot of Battery Hill, which was bulldozed away in the 1940s to make room for the shipyard's wartime growth. A rail line was later built below the fence on the left. The photographer is looking up the harbour toward the spot where the Harvey A. Veniot causeway now crosses the harbour. When the land for the town was deeded to Deacon John Patterson in 1787, a forty-foot swathe along the waterfront was reserved for a road—Front Street. Patterson laid out the other streets in straight lines and square lots, but where they met Front Street the lots had odd shapes. Any buildings standing today on the harbour side of this road, except the Customs House, are on made land.

THE TRADERS PROCESSION, 1895

A photographer set up at the eastern end of Market Square to capture the 1895 Traders Procession making its way along Water Street. Horse-drawn parade floats represented the town's various businesses—note the large scissors on a tailor's float near the rear of the procession, possibly advertising J. Smith Grant's haberdashery. The four-storey building on the left of the unpaved street is E. S. Brown's harness shop, later the site of the Golden Boat restaurant. The gabled building on this side of it, now the site of the deCoste Entertainment Centre, held a tinsmith and candy store, with living quarters upstairs. McKenna's tobacco factory was behind the store, toward the harbour. The nearer buildings—a furniture store, bakery, meat shop, and grocery store—are also gone. The stone house at the right, built about 1824, is now a lawyer's office. The stone building past it, out of sight in this photo, was built in 1825 of random stone and once housed the Mercantile Bank. Sheriff William Harris left it for use as a museum when he died in 1965, but it was turned into a shop. The museum didn't materialize, and it was turned into a shop. The other stone building dates to 1824, and is now a shop.

THE CUSTOMS HOUSE, 1896

In 1874 the windmill on Windmill Hill, which had been there since about 1790, was demolished by the Dominion Government to make room for a Customs House. Increased shipping traffic through Pictou created a need to collect tariffs and customs duties, and to regulate the flow of goods and people through one of Canada's most significant points of entry. The DG, as the government was frequently referred to, also provided offices in the new building for a harbour master and installed a tower with navigational lights. The brick-lined basement was designed to hold casks of liquor in bond, while awaiting payment of duties. There was also a stone sink for draining confiscated alcohol during the 1898–1929 Prohibition. InterColonial Railway cars can be seen on the tracks running behind the customs house, as can the masts of sailing ships. The railway station was to the right of the photo at this time, but a new station was built on a site to the left in 1905. The eleven-foot ceilings and seven marble fireplaces contributed to the building's conversion to an inn in the late 1990s.

OLD POST OFFICE, 1896

Pictou's fortress-like post office, on the north side of Water Street in an area known as the Burnt Ruins because of a previous fire at the site, was built of heavy stone blocks in 1895. The construction date and the letters VR, for Victoria Regina, were carved over the two small windows on the front dormer. The building sported an unusual feature—a window in the chimney that gained it a spot in the Ripley's Believe It or Not newspaper column. Prior to the construction of the post office, the Postmaster Edmund MacPhail operated from the ground floor of the Young Men's Christian Association (YMCA) building across George Street, on the left in this photo. The old post office closed in 1955 when it was replaced by a new, one-storey brick building on Front Street. A Pictou East post office was established temporarily in Victory Heights in 1943 to serve the increased population there.

COUNTY COURTHOUSE, 1899

A crowd gathered at the ornate county courthouse, on the corner of Willow and Church streets, in early March, 1899, to celebrate the end of the Boer siege of the South African town of Ladysmith. Built in 1858, the courthouse featured exterior carving by Peter Cormick, elaborate interior plasterwork, an arched ceiling over the raised judge's bench, and a three-piece stained-glass window showing the blindfolded goddess of Justice. The lock on the front door was dated 1779. The courthouse was the scene of many dramatic cases, including the 1893 trial of Joseph Dunn and William Doyle, who robbed Douglas' tailor shop; and of Westville miners Welsh and Kent, sentenced to four years in Dorchester penitentiary for blowing apart a jewellery store safe. The evidence against them included asbestos from the safe on their boots, and stolen jewellery found in their rooms. The courthouse remained in use until the Justice Building opened on Water Street on November 21, 1986. Designated as municipal heritage property, the old building burned on September 15, 1987, before a new use for it could be found. The stained glass windows were saved and stored, but the ruin could not be rebuilt, and it was demolished on November 25, 1987.

THE OLD ROAD, 1900

Now called Haliburton Road, the Old Road, or Halifax Road, was the route of choice for people travelling by land to Pictou when the town was young. It followed the shore up the West River to Durham, beyond Mount Thom to Truro, and then on to Windsor or Halifax. Here, the traveller is on the hill where the Sutherland Harris Memorial Hospital now stands, and the Pictou Academy tower is in sight on the left. Haliburton Road is now a wide, paved street, but in 1900 it was a rutted track with a footpath on one side. A 1935 bequest from Pictou Advocate editor John Fisher provided money to pave the road for a few hundred metres, beginning at the Norway House gate. In 1947 the broken surface was removed and the Nova Scotia government paved the road's entire length.

THE GUT BRIDGE, 1900

Deacon John Patterson built the first bridge across the Town Gut in 1800, paying for it from his own pocket. The bridge rested on vertical pillars, costing Patterson sixty pounds. He billed the town, but on his death in 1808 he was still owed fifty pounds. The bridge was swept away in the 1873 August Gale, and the town spent $115.60 to repair the structure, possibly assuming that the expense took care of the account. In the mid-1900s the province built a new bridge and re-routed the road to join the new traffic circle—the Pictou Rotary—under construction near Hockin's Corner. The farm on the left, now the Cyr property, was operated about 1900 by the Mahar family, which sold meat from the premises. Note the signs placed on the wooden walls of the one-lane bridge.

SAW MILL BROOK, 1900

Daniel MacKenzie, from Invernesshire in Scotland, settled a few miles west of the Town Gut about 1774. He took over a sawmill established in 1769 by William Kennedy, a settler from Truro, on the edge of a brook flowing into Pictou Harbour. Kennedy's sawmill was the first in Pictou County, as well as the first frame building. He sold out in 1774 and returned to Truro, later becoming the first settler in Stewiacke. This photo of Saw Mill Brook—now part of Lyons Brook—was taken around 1900. Pictou enjoyed a flourishing timber trade with Europe prior to a British economic depression in 1825–26, when lumber prices dropped. The trade gradually revived, but most of the large trees near the shore had been culled by then. The new mining industry created a demand for pit props, and a revival in shipbuilding bolstered the timber trade.

VIEW FROM CUSTOMS HOUSE TOWER, 1905

Chapel Street runs up the hill on the left of this 1905 photo taken from the Customs House tower, facing northeast. The street was so named because the first Roman Catholic church, St. Patrick's, later known as St. George's, was on Chapel Street. The East End school tower is seen at the top of this photograph, and Stella Maris Roman Catholic Church, which replaced St. Patrick's/St. George's when the congregation grew, is on the right. The treed park in the foreground became the site of the new post office in 1955. The lane on the left enters the railway station, then a year old, from Front Street. It and a roundhouse were built on land "made" by filling in a cove between the Customs House and Battery Hill. There are planks across the ditches along Chapel Street, down which rainwater ran into the harbour.

BATTERY PARK, 1905

In 1812, the province bought the property for the Pictou battery from Edward Mortimer for £163. The intent was to use the promontory to protect the harbour from Fenian raids. The cannons were cast at a Spanish factory and sent initially to Halifax. Pictou got them as hand-me-downs in 1865, but they were never fired in conflict. The site was a popular spot to view Pictou harbour, and was kept as a park in the early 1900s. In the early 1940s, 40,000 cubic yards of earth were removed from the hill to make room for wartime shipbuilding, and the cannons went to the salvage mill. The biggest one was saved, and given to J. F. MacKenzie of Caribou Island. It was passed to Andrew Gunn of Pictou, and in 1964 to Kenneth Hopps, to display at his museum at Lowden's Beach, Braeshore. With the museum's closure, the guns were sent to Halifax, but came back to storage in Pictou in 2003, where they await placement on the lawn of the Royal Canadian Legion, next to the big anchor there.

LOOKING WEST ON CHURCH STREET, 1908

A horse and wagon wait patiently on Church Street in 1908. The nearest house on the right was the Heighton home, with Bowes' store beside it. Next is Lorrain's Hotel, built in 1820 by Pictou stonemason John Lorrain as an inn and tavern. The Pictou Masonic Lodge met here, and it was a stop for the Halifax stagecoach. St. Andrew's Day was celebrated at the Inn with as many as twenty-nine toasts, each accompanied by a song and prodigious drinking. Revellers began with a toast to Scotland's patron saint, then past and current royalty, Scotland, various governors, soldiers, clergy, sundry economic interests, Robert Burns, Walter Scott, and always ended with a toast to the chief magistrate. Carroll's livery service, just down the hill, would pick up the revellers at dawn and take them home.

FRONT STREET, LOOKING WEST, 1912

The photographer is looking west on Front Street, facing Munro's photographic studio at the end of the street on the left. Next to it on a Coleraine Street building is a sign saying *Ciad Mile Failte* (Gaelic for "one hundred thousand welcomes"). Looming over them on the right is the Shamrock tobacco sign on the side of the St. Julian Hotel. The welcome sign and decorations on the storefronts indicate this photo was taken during an important event, perhaps just after the parade on Front Street in honor of the Duke of Connaught's 1912 visit to Pictou. The cart on the left has "Baggage" written on its back, and was probably making a delivery from the nearby wharf to one of the hotels along Front Street.

TWO STEEPLES AND A SCHOOL, 1905

This westerly shot from the Customs House tower captures the intersection of Depot and Front streets. The Wallace Hotel, across from Depot Street, was the town's largest at the time. Just a half-block from the railway station and docks, the sixty-three-room hotel could seat forty-eight in its dining room, and offered a parlour, lounge, and writing room. Fire destroyed many of the buildings shown, and the Wallace Hotel site is now occupied by a take-out restaurant and a parking lot for the Highlander Pub on Twining Street. The Dominion Hotel, later a private home which burned and was rebuilt in the 1990s, is on the left side of Chapel Street, on the right of the photo at the top. The spires of St. Andrew's Kirk, left, and St. James Anglican, near the centre, have been altered: the former due to a 2000 lightning strike, and the latter following a 1954 hurricane. The tower of the East End School, on the right, disappeared from the horizon when it was torn down and a new school was built at the same site in 1930.

HARBOUR TOWN, 1905

Ships' passengers entering Pictou from the Northumberland Strait before 1900 would have, as their first clue that there was a fair-sized town nestled in the harbour, a starboard view of the cradle used to hold large boats under construction, and a host of wharves reaching seaward. Rounding Battery Hill, church steeples and school bell towers would come into view, with more details appearing as their ship neared shore. Here, Pictou Academy, on the horizon on the left, looms over the Patterson home at the top of Deacon's Hill. St. Andrew's Kirk spire rises above the G. J. Hamilton and Sons sign on the back of the St. Julian Hotel, next door to the biscuit company's first plant at the corner of Water and Coleraine streets. The public slip is at the bottom right corner of the photo, at the foot of Coleraine Street.

PICTOU LANDING, 1905

Across the harbour from Pictou was Fishers Grant, named after the original grantee, John Fisher. It was renamed Pictou Landing after the railway line was built from New Glasgow to the spot in 1867. Rail passengers had to be ferried across the harbour to Pictou wharves to continue their journey by ship to destinations around the Northumberland Strait, Quebec, the Atlantic coast, or across the Atlantic. An 1879 business directory listed twenty-four men living in Pictou Landing, but did not count wives and children. Most of them worked for the railway or the ferry business, and there was one hotel, three stores, a post office, a telegraph office, a Justice of the Peace, and a smithy. The Pictou Landing First Nation reserve is a separate community from this, situated to the left of the photo, at the seaward side of the sandbar at the harbour entrance.

BARRY'S MILL BRIDGE, 1905

A child in breeches perches at the end of the new steel truss bridge that replaced an earlier, fragile wooden structure spanning Barry's Brook, above Alfred Barry's millpond. The provincial government installed hundreds of the single-lane structures, which have a life expectancy of about 100 years, between 1880 and 1940. Many of them still stand, but this bridge was replaced in the 1960s by a culvert and a built-up roadbed with two lanes of pavement, on Highway Six, laid on top. The house in the photo, at the entrance to Haliburton cemetery, was torn down in the late 1900s. Just a few kilometres from downtown Pictou, the millpond was considered a beauty spot and was popular with anglers and picnickers in summer, and skaters in winter.

BEACHES ROAD, 1905

Pictou photographer William Munro thought Beaches Road, also known as Beeches Road, was a beautiful spot, and he took many photos of the route to the golf links and to Braeshore. Some Pictou residents apparently didn't agree with his perspective, as local officials placed the hospital for infectious disease three miles from town along the shore, accessible by this road. The public gallows were set up near the infectious hospital. In his memoirs, Pictou policeman Peachie Carroll recalls watching a murderer, riding to the gallows along this road in 1864, sitting up in a coffin carried in a horse-drawn cart. Carroll was four years old at the time, following hundreds of others to watch the hanging.

WATER STREET, 1910

A brass band leads a parade westward on Water Street, about 1910. The two nearest buildings on the left are gone, replaced by the Nova Scotia Liquor Store, later becoming the Grohmann Knives factory and store. The Shamrock tobacco sign is on the far side of Market Square, and the Pictou theatre, known at this time as the Advocate Hall and recognized by its bowed front, can be seen just past it. A Mr. B. Gravestock bought the building in 1915 and refurbished it to seat five hundred people and an eight-member orchestra. During renovations, while movies were shown at the curlers' rink, the movie projector was stolen. A crooked fingerprint left on a window helped track the machine, but the culprit escaped. The theatre site is now occupied by a hardware store, and the Pictou County Justice Building, home of Supreme, provincial, and family courts, is directly across the street.

WATERING TROUGHS, 1912

In this undated photo, two men pose by the horse trough at the intersection of Church and Water streets. There were three public horse troughs listed in town records, filled by springs. Another was at Wellington and Denoon streets, and a third site was unidentified in town records. As well as providing drinks for horses, the primary mode of land travel prior to 1900, this trough also served as a washing place for travellers entering the town from the Old Road. With the advent of gas-powered automobiles, both known troughs were deemed surplus to requirements and removed by 1946. Haliburton Street is behind the men, and the large house on the left is Professor Singleton's Pictou School of Music, now an apartment building.

PICTOU TOWN HALL, 1920

A man trudges past Pictou Town Hall on Church Street in 1920, while horse-powered low delivery sleighs await their drivers. Before it was taken over by the town, this building had been the first county courthouse, replaced in 1858 with the more ornate building down the street. The county jail, a separate facility, was situated behind the new county courthouse. The building shown here had cells in the basement, replacing the town's first jail, built in 1792. Three tiny cells were designated for women, but they were more often used for solitary confinement of men. One was taken to the town dump in 1973 to hold stray dogs. The town hall burned on July 21, 1985, and town administration moved to the Collins Building on Water Street, a twentieth-century building which had been restored after a fire started in a restaurant on the main floor. After the 1985 fire, offenders in temporary need of cell space were locked up at the courthouse and, later, at the new RCMP detachment on Caladh Avenue. Church Street Villa, an apartment complex for seniors, was built on this site in 1986. The windowed building seen to the left of the Town Hall was the George Street meeting place of the Great War Veterans Association.

OVERVIEW OF PICTOU, 1923

This 1923 aerial shot could very well have been taken when airplanes visited Pictou from the United States during that year's *Hector* anniversary celebrations, offering rides for a fee. It shows Battery Hill in the bottom centre, its cannons the black dots in a semi-circle in the middle of the hill. Left of it is the railway roundhouse, and to the right is the shipyard. The foundry is above the roundhouse. Stella Maris church is in the photo's centre, and the water tower is near the top of the photo at the centre. Pictou Academy is in the top left corner, and near it is the wireless station and mast, built about 1919 by the Marconi Wireless Telegraph Company to communicate with the Magdalen Islands, because much of the Quebec islands' goods and services funneled through Pictou. Operators, including Thomas H. Raddall, Fred Hughes, Joe Maloney, and George Moore, boarded at Kenny John MacKenzie's slip. Dismantled in 1924, the mast was sold to the fish processing company, Maritime Packers, and the building used as a ticket office for the Pictou North Colchester exhibition.

ABANDONED DREDGE, 1938

This harbour dredge was left to rust after it went aground on shallow water and soft mud in 1925, about 120 metres from the grain mill, seen in the background on the Pictou shore. It was a popular target for harbour swimmers, and legend has it that liquor smugglers used it as a cache. The crane and steel bucket rusted and fell into the harbour—not hitting any swimmers—but the machinery remained. A member of the 1937 Pictou Academy graduating class rowed out to the site in the middle of the night with three sticks of dynamite, intent on destroying the eyesore, but police intercepted him. The dredge was gradually removed over the years. An 1827 drawing shows a ballast wharf in the harbour, but it was further east, closer to Market Wharf, and used for ships to offload their ballast rock before loading timber.

170 YEARS OF PROGRESS, 1940

The Pictou recreation centre can be seen at the top left of this late 1940s aerial view. Down the hill from it is Central School, later known as Dawson School, which was demolished in 2003 after closing in favour of a new school on Wellington Street. G. J. Hamilton and Sons is at the bottom left, across the railway tracks from the Irving Oil tanks. The Irving family of New Brunswick donated this property to the town in 1990 for construction of the ship *Hector* replica, Hector Interpretive Centre, and Quay. Many of the businesses lining the east side of Coleraine Street, running in front of St. Andrew's Kirk, and Front Street, at right angles to Coleraine, were lost to fire after this photo was made. The park at the corner of Depot and Front streets, in front of the Customs House, was cleared in 1955 to make room for the new post office. Municipal politicians pointed to the concentration of commerce shown in this photo when they promoted redevelopment of the downtown in the 1990s.

Chapter 2

A Place for People

PRINCE ALBERT'S WELCOMING COMMITTEE, 1860

Prominent Pictou citizens were selected to welcome Prince Albert, Prince of Wales and later King Edward VII, when he stopped in Pictou during his 1860 tour of Canada. A newspaper of the time referred to the white guests as "ladies and gentlemen," but the Mi'kmaq in attendance were called "children of the forest." Among the gentlemen gathered outside the courthouse on August 11, are from the left, Major Benjamin Hammett Norton, the American consul; William Brownrigg, a boot and shoe maker; Robert Patterson Grant, later vice-president of the Pictou Bank and member of the Nova Scotia assembly; Judge W. A. Henry; Clarence Primrose of Primrose Brothers merchants and bankers; Pictou Academy treasurer James Crichton (also spelled Creighton); William

Gordon, merchant; James Primrose, of Primrose Brothers; A. P. Ross; W. H. Davies, owner and operator of Pictou Foundry; Robert Doull, a merchant and ship-owner who was later member of Parliament; Hon. James MacDonald; barrister Martin I. Wilkins; Howard Primrose, of Primrose Brothers; Dr. James Skinner; John Crerar, a justice of the peace, merchant and ship owner; and Dan Dickson, secretary of Haliburton Cemetery Company. As founding directors of the Pictou bank in 1874, Grant, Gordon, Doull, and Crerar, along with other shareholders, later lost three-quarters of their initial $500,000 capital investment when the enterprise failed in 1886. Gordon, Ross, and Grant were also members of the town's board of health which, in 1848, had overseen the construction of a hospital to treat sailors arriving in the port with infectious diseases.

J. D. B. FRASER, c.1865

James Daniel Bain Fraser was the first to produce chloroform in Nova Scotia, at his Pictou drugstore in 1848. Sir James Young Simpson, a University of Edinburgh obstetrics professor, devised the chemical in 1847 as a safe pain relief during childbirth. Fraser experimented with Simpson's scant instructions for the drug, and gave it to his wife when she delivered their son, Robert Peter, on March 22, 1848. Although Fraser is credited with being the first in Canada to use the anesthesia during childbirth, there is evidence that a Dr. Worthington in Quebec beat him to it in January, 1848. Fraser made chloroform to supply Halifax doctors. The first to use it was Dr. W. J. Almon, who gave it to a woman from the poorhouse in March, 1848, when he amputated her thumb. He used it next to amputate another poorhouse resident's leg. Fraser was also interested in coal chemistry, taking out a search licence near Albion Mines and finding the seam of stellar coal that gave Stellarton its name. He was a member of Pictou's Literary and Scientific Society in the 1830s and 1840s, researched the properties of creosote, and ran for the Tories in the 1830 Brandy Election. He died in 1869.

MARY MICKLE HENDERSON, 1816–1890, AND CHILD

In 1836, at twenty years of age, Mary Mickle Henderson married William Black Henderson, and emigrated from Scotland to Pictou with him and their two eldest children—and not much else. Over the next thirty years she bore and raised eight more children, six of them girls, at the tall house on Water Street, across from what is now the Grohmann Knives factory. One daughter, Rowena, born in 1859, grew up to marry Pictou detective Peachie Carroll. In Mary's day, women did not usually have paid employment, and if they did it ceased when they married. At home, they worked hard. There was no electricity, no indoor plumbing, and all food was cooked from scratch in heavy iron pots and pans on a stove that needed constant tending. Women heated the water for laundry on the wood or coal stove, and washed clothes by hand in a big tub. Frequently they had to make the soap as well. Two or three irons were heated on the hot stove surface, so the one in use could be exchanged when it cooled. Well-off families could have clothing made for them, but most women would sew cotton flour and sugar bags into underwear and nightclothes. Families ate a lot of mackerel, herring, potatoes and eggs, and women started their bread at night to bake early in the morning.

THE KING OF PICTOU'S BIG HOUSE, 1890

Edward Mortimer was born in Banffshire, Scotland, in 1767, and travelled to Pictou in 1788 on a trading mission. He stayed, married Squire Robert Patterson's daughter, Sarah, made a fortune in lumber and shipping, and threw his support behind Pictou Academy founder Thomas McCulloch, the Reform Party (later the Liberals) and the Presbyterian secessionists. He won Pictou County's first election in 1799. Mortimer's political involvement, popularity, and considerable wealth earned him the nicknames "King of Pictou" and "Oat Meal Emperor from the East." In 1810 he hired a crew of stonemasons and carpenters from Scotland to build this mansion, Stone House, at Norway (or Mortimer's) Point, at a reported cost of ten thousand pounds sterling. During its four years of construction, Mortimer established a shipping and mercantile firm with George Smith of Pictou and William Liddell of New Glasgow, and was known as a generous man. When Mortimer died in 1819, at fifty-one, his estate was insolvent. The home and a pension were left to his wife, who lived at the Stone House until 1835.

PRIMROSE MILL, 1886

The Primrose brothers—Howard, Clarence, and James—built this mill west of Battery Hill in 1845 to grind grain, saw lumber, and card wool. By 1880 they had established themselves as innovators, being the first Pictonians to use steam power in manufacturing. They were thriving Water Street merchants and bankers, and James and Clarence owned an elegant home on St. Andrews Street, Terrace Cottage, which was used as an annex for the Braeside Inn after 1935, and then demolished. Under the name Primrose Brothers, the company went on to obtain large tracts of lumber in Colchester and Queens counties by 1900, employing hundreds of men in winter to cut wood for export to Europe. The company's tobacco factory produced Pictou Twist, so-called because of its appearance. It was later taken over by their foreman, a McKenna. The Primroses also ran a brickyard on the River John Road. Clarence became a Senator, and his son, James Primrose, served as mayor for five terms. A grandson of the family, Philip C. H. Primrose, was one of the first members of the North West Mounted Police, later the RCMP. He served throughout the west and in the Klondike gold rush, was made a superintendent in 1899, and re-organized the force's criminal investigation branch in 1913. He was an Edmonton magistrate from 1915–1935, and made lieutenant governor of Alberta in 1936. He died six months later. A railway roundhouse built on the mill site in 1887 is now long gone, and there are no longer any Primroses in Pictou.

MACKENZIE HOME, C.1890

John MacKenzie had stonemasons Robert Hogg and his son John Hogg, from Dumfriesshire in Scotland, build this elegant mansion at Sawmill Brook (now Lyons Brook), a few miles west of Pictou, in 1831.

MacKenzie had inherited Mill Brook Farm from his father, Daniel, who had operated a sawmill there fifty years earlier. Stone for the house came from a quarry, owned by John MacKenzie and his brother Charles, on the edge of Sawmill Brook. The stone was shipped to Charlottetown to build Province House in 1834–37. The house, which had a brick extension added in the early 1900s, remained in the family for 150 years.

PEACHIE AND DITTO 1895

Peter Owen (Peachie) Carroll was born in Pictou in 1860, the son of Peter and Mary Grace Carroll. Peachie's maternal grandfather, John Pagan of Greenock, Scotland, was a principal in the Philadelphia Company, and owner of the brig *Hector* that brought settlers to Pictou in 1773. Like most Pictou boys, Peachie attended the Academy, worked in his father's business, and went to sea aboard both fishing and cargo schooners. He worked in the mining and smelting towns of the American West and hunted gold in the Klondike, but his greatest claim to fame was as a detective. He was police chief in Nelson, B.C, as well as Pictou and Yarmouth, and served with the railway, mining company, and provincial police forces. Peachie was called to cases all over the Maritimes. He is photographed here with his friend William "Ditto" Dalton, owner of the Red Onion bar on South Market Street. Peachie was married three times and had four children. He died in 1933.

THE RED ONION, C.1895

The man with folded arms is Red Onion proprietor William "Ditto" Dalton, on the doorstep of his 1890s business. The small South Market Street watering hole had a large reputation as a gathering place for sporting men, interested in horse racing, dog racing and fighting, singing, and games of chance. The Red Onion walls were lined with photographs and curios from all over the world, and Dalton kept pigeons, fighting roosters, dogs, and a tightrope-walking goat. Prohibition in 1898 closed the bar, but through a quirk in the legislation, Dalton was able to import booze from Halifax, where its sale and delivery to anyone in Nova Scotia were legal. Meanwhile liquor retailers in the rest of the province had to succumb to the lobbying of a strong temperance movement. The Red Onion survived an 1890 fire that destroyed Market Wharf and the lock-up across the street, killing an imprisoned sailor. The Red Onion building burned in the 1950s.

DITTO AND HIS TIGHTROPE-WALKING GOAT, 1895

THOMAS LATHER'S SEASIDE HOME, 1895

At one time, Thomas Lather was a captain of one of the finest schooners that ever sailed from Gloucester, Mass. In his later years, he lived aboard this abandoned schooner, which was hauled up high and dry on the shore near the Pictou Iron Foundry, across the cove from the customs house, seen here in the background. Capt. Lather caught perch in the harbour to sell to townsfolk. Other unusual Pictou characters of the late 1800s were clockmaker Thomas Moody, a familiar figure on town streets; Dick Jackson, who lived on the Cape John Road and kept his hair in elaborate shoulder-length curls; Pope Hatton, the weigher at the old market scales; Long Hector MacLean, who could bite a nail in two; Bouge Dhu, who lived under an upturned boat in summer and in country barns in winter; and Gregor Ochard, of whom small boys were frightened.

BOBBY SUTHERLAND, 1875

Bobby Sutherland was a semi-recluse who lived in a cabin three miles from town on Beaches Road, on property next to the hospital for infectious diseases. The earlier studio photo was taken about 1875, while the later one, c.1895, shows his small cabin and the implements hung about the place. The remains of the cabin's foundation are still visible. In the 1880s, a handful of Pictou boys would visit Bobby Sutherland on summer Saturday afternoons, running along beside Billy Munro, a disabled boy who drove a four-wheeled cart pulled by two big dogs. In his memoirs, Detective Peachie Carroll recalls that one of the dogs, named Nemo, would dive in the harbour to retrieve rocks from the bottom.

BOBBY SUTHERLAND AT HOME, 1895 (BELOW)

THE SIR JOHN WILLIAM DAWSON HOUSE, c.1900

This modest wooden building at the corner of Church and Constitution streets, at the foot of Deacon's Hill, was the 1820 birthplace of Sir John William Dawson. Educated at Pictou Academy and the University of Edinburgh, Dawson became interested in geology during his 1842 tour of Nova Scotia with noted geologist Sir Charles Lyell. Dawson lectured at Dalhousie University and established Truro Normal College, for teachers' training, in 1854. He was Nova Scotia's first superintendent of education, pioneering free schools in Nova Scotia. He was the first president of the Royal Society of Canada, the first to study fossils in coal, and he became principal of McGill University and its natural history professor in 1855, and founded its teaching college, of which he was the first principal, in 1857. Dawson, who preferred to be called William rather than John, opposed the theory of evolution, arguing that science supported the biblical version of creation. He was knighted in 1884, and died in Montreal in 1899. His son, George Mercer Dawson, was also a noted geologist and the namesake for Dawson City, Yukon Territory. The house was demolished in the 1940s, and a monument to the Dawson father and son placed on the site in 1961.

SIR J. WILLIAM DAWSON, 1890

The Crerar family's Glenalmond, c.1900

Capt. William Crerar built his house Glenalmond of ship's ballast rock on the hilltop overlooking the small cove called the Town Gut in 1877. He was one of seven tall sons of Peter and Anne Crerar, who arrived in Pictou from Glenalmond, Scotland, in 1817. Although he had never seen a train, Peter designed and built Canada's first railway between Albion Mines, now Stellarton, and the Abercrombie coal pier. He also designed St. James Anglican Church in Pictou, and many bridges in northern Nova Scotia. The family established as a seafaring and shipbuilding enterprise, owning five ships named *Wolfe*, among others. One son, Capt. Daniel, died in a Shanghai hospital in 1859; his brother, Capt. Ewan, died with twenty-one crew members on January 19, 1857, when the *Lord Ashburton* wrecked on Grand Manan Island while en route to New Brunswick from France. Capt. Peter, Jr, a merchant, shipbuilder, and seafarer, died in Wales in 1868. James, the only non-seafaring brother, practised medicine briefly in River John before becoming a British army surgeon in the Crimean War. He died in Britain. Capt. David married an American and built a home on Willow Street, where he lived the rest of his life. Capt. John, president of the ill-fated Pictou Bank, also lived on Willow Street, as well as in Halifax and England, but he died at Glenalmond in 1889. On William's death, the property went to his nephews, and then changed hands several times. Crumbling mortar led to the home being torn down in the 1960s.

LORD STRATHCONA AT NORWAY HOUSE, 1909

Edward Mortimer's Stone House changed hands several times after his wife sold it in 1853, before Lord Strathcona, Donald Alexander Smith, Chief Factor of the Hudson's Bay Company, bought it in 1880. He renamed it Norway House after a Hudson's Bay Company outpost in the Northwest Territories. Lord Strathcona was the man who drove the last spike in Canada's first transcontinental railway, at Craigellachie, British Columbia, in 1885. He had arrived in Canada fifty years earlier, educated but penniless, to work for the Hudson's Bay Company counting rat skins for about forty dollars a year. By the time of this 1890 photo at Norway Point, he had stately homes in Montreal and Winnipeg, this "summer home" in Pictou, and assets worth more than nine million dollars. Norway Point was sold in 1918 to the International Order of Odd Fellows for use as an orphanage and nursing home. After a new nursing home was built next door, Norway House was sold and turned into an inn. The building is said to be haunted by ghosts from a previous home at the site.

ORANGE PARADE ON WATER STREET, 1910

The Pictou True Blue Lodge No. 32, the local branch of the Orange Order, was organized in July of 1877, and owned a hall on South Market Street. The group met the first and third Tuesdays of each month. A large contingent of Orangemen is shown here parading west on Water Street and turning up Willow Street. The Orange Order, named after William III of England and prince of Orange in southeast France, was founded in northern Ireland in 1795 to support a Protestant monarchy in England. In 1901 Canada had an estimated Orange membership of 200,000, increasing to 350,000 by 1914. It was estimated that one-third of Protestant men belonged to the Orange Order in the years leading up to World War One, but their patriotism led them to sign up for military service in droves, and many died overseas. The picket fence on the left surrounds the current site of the Pictou County cenotaph, built after World War One.

THE TOBIN HOME Jeweller Frank J. Tobin, known as the harp player of Pictou because of the large instrument he kept in his hallway, moved to the town in 1892 to open a Water Street jewellery, watch making, and engraving business. He lived in this large home on Front Street. Originally from Bridgewater, he first worked for Eastwood jewellers in New Glasgow in 1888, then set up a business in Truro with another man, and finally moved to Pictou. He was the first in Pictou to sell phonographs, the first to bring in an Edison recorder with double-thick records, and the first to sell diamond needles. Every day at noon he gave the correct time to the chief telephone operator, Dolly MacNeill, who would sound the siren on the roof of the Church Street fire station. The practice had a twofold goal—to test the siren and to provide the correct time to townspeople. Tobin retired in 1941 and his business bought by David Neima, who moved to New Glasgow when Pictou's wartime boom ended. Tobin would drive around town accompanied by a miniature dog in a Scottish costume, with a pipe in its mouth.

PICTOU COUNTY JAIL, 1912

SHERIFF HARRIS THE SIXTH (THIRD FROM LEFT)

The Pictou County jail, immortalized in the Haggerty Brothers' 1970s song "Thirty Days in Pictou County Jail," was built in 1891 under the eagle eye of Sheriff J. Simpson (Sim) Harris, the fifth in the Harris sheriff dynasty. The first Sheriff Harris was Thomas, a nephew of Dr. John Harris, who arrived courtesy of the Philadelphia Company in 1775. John's son John Washington Harris succeeded his cousin Thomas in 1811, and served for forty-six years. Under him the first courthouse and jail were built on Church Street, which were taken over by the town of Pictou upon its incorporation. The third Sheriff Harris was John W.'s son William Henry Harris, who served from 1857 to 1881. George S. Harris succeeded his father in 1881, serving until 1885, when Sim Harris took over. He served for forty-nine years, sharing the duties with his son, William H. (the second) as he grew older. W. H. Harris took over as the sixth Sheriff Harris when his father died in 1934. He is the tall, bespectacled man, shown here with Judge Welsford MacDonald, Edward MacDonald, Pictou Academy principal C. L. Moore, court stenographer Isabel Whitman, Charles A. Manning, and three unidentified men. The six Harrises carried out five executions during their collective time in office.

A Place for People

A PRINCE'S VISIT, 1912

A crowd met Prince Arthur, Duke of Connaught and Governor General of Canada, when he stepped ashore from SS *Earl Grey* on July 31, 1912. Among the dignitaries were the local Member of Parliament E. MacDonald, Legislative Assembly members R. MacGregor, R. MacKay and C. Tanner, Pictou county warden J. MacKay, Trenton Mayor J. Strickland, New Glasgow Mayor John Underwood, Stellarton Mayor D. B. Rogers, and Pictou Mayor James Primrose. The children sang The Maple Leaf Forever and presented flowers to the Duchess of Connaught and her daughter, Princess Patricia. Note the smoke at the top of Battery Hill, from the cannons fired in salute by Pictou volunteers. The royal party toured Pictou and the surrounding countryside before re-boarding SS *Earl Grey* that evening and sailing away.

MCCULLOCH MEMORIALIZED, 1912

One of the Duke of Connaught's tasks on his 1912 visit was to dedicate a tablet at the "old college," as the first Pictou Academy building on Church Street was known, honouring the school's founder, Rev. Dr. Thomas McCulloch, and its illustrious graduate Sir J. William Dawson. Dr. Thomas McCulloch founded the academy in 1816 to educate students of all denominations and to provide the community with future candidates for the ministry. He battled a pro-Anglican political bias in the provincial and national governments, and a schism within his own Presbyterian church, to achieve his dream of establishing a degree-granting institution in Pictou. The academy was never allowed to confer degrees, but its students, including renowned scientist and educator Sir J. William Dawson, made their marks around the world. The houses shown across Church Street from the school still stand, but the school was torn down in 1932, and Pictou's fire hall was later built on the site. A monument marks the school site.

The Stalker Building, 1912

John A. Stalker built this grand brick edifice on Coleraine Street, facing the intersection with Water Street, in 1876–77. He and his son Alex, who was later a stipendiary magistrate and a fire chief like his father, operated a bank, a crockery and home decorating store, and a grocery in the building at different times. Crockery imprinted with the J. A. Stalker name is considered a find in today's antique shops. The Stalker families of John A., James H., and Alex were all listed in an 1879 directory as living in the large building. John Stalker also built and outfitted the Pictou Bank, now Scotiabank, next door. John died in 1907 at sixty-five, and his wife, Sarah Hogg, left Pictou in 1923 to live with their daughter Anna Murray in California. James, whose daughter Georgina married biscuit factory heir Howard Hamilton, ran an import business on Church Street. The Stalker building was later used as apartments, an insurance office, and the town's library and became an inn in the 1990s.

YOUNG PROFESSIONALS, 1915

A group of young men posed for this 1915 studio portrait by Pictou photographer William Munro. On the left are druggists James Murdock and W. I. Fergusson, who operated a pharmacy in the building which had formerly housed Hamilton's biscuit factory at the corner of Coleraine and Water streets. The same building is now a health and beauty spa. Next is Dr. George A. Dunn, who attended the delivery of the Sutherland Memorial Hospital's first baby, Clara Sutherland Cheverie, in 1928. James W. J. Bethune, next, opened MacDonald and Bethune Dry Goods in 1916 by buying out Thomas Glover's, established on Water Street in 1872. On the right is A. Corbett MacDonald, who operated the John R. MacDonald Grocery Store on Market Square, which was started by his father.

PICTOU STUDENTS, c.1925

A group of Pictou students poses by an unidentified school, possibly in New Glasgow during a field trip, about 1925. Front, from the left, are Max Murdoch, unknown, "Pin" Ferguson, unknown, "Brud" MacLeod, Donnie MacMillan, two unknowns, Lew Munsie. Back, from the left, are Arnold Clarke, unknown, Allie Emery, unknown, Chester Roach, unknown, Bill Ives, unknown, Jim Murray.

Extracurricular activities for children of the late 1800s and early 1900s included hunting rabbits and fishing, swimming in the harbour, hockey on the frozen harbour, Sheriff's Pond, or the pond at Belleville Farm, (now the golf course). They played marbles, caught tadpoles, and attended cadets and Boy Scouts. There were always chores, some unheard of today, and most to be completed before walking to up to two miles to school each day. They split and carried firewood, dragged coal to the kitchen stove, helped with gardening and animal care, emptied chamber pots and cleaned outhouses, made beds and carried water. In school, as well as reading, writing and arithmetic, they studied Latin, scriptures, and natural history—what we would call science today. The boys entered Pictou Academy by one door, and the girls by another. If they misbehaved, they had to stand in the corner or, for severe infractions, get struck with a pointer or a strap. They often wore hand-me-down clothing, and five cents was a fortune. When they became adults, they mourned the good old days of their childhood.

RED ONION FRIENDS, 1928

When the Red Onion burned, this late-1920s photograph was rescued, along with some other curios and pictures. Most of the men here are unknown, but the little boy in the middle is a very young Alfred "Boo" Dalton, the son of Red Onion proprietor William "Ditto" Dalton. Alfred later moved to Scotch Hill, where he lived to old age. The man to his left is a McLaren, of the family that owned Pictou's funeral home, and one of the other men is a Heighton. Among the other scorched items retrieved was a photo of Prince Edward Island's first female driver, a copy of the pedigree for one of "Ditto's" prize dogs, a song book, a puppet head used in the Red Onion's Punch and Judy shows, and some unidentified photos.

DEACON PATTERSON'S COTTAGE, 1938

When this photo of Deacon John Patterson's house was taken, the small frame building was already 150 years old and the oldest standing house in Pictou. Known as "Father of Pictou," *Hector* passenger John Patterson was granted 250 acres at what is now the centre of town. After marrying Anne Harris, the daughter of *Betsey* settler Matthew Harris, he built this house in 1788 at the top of what is now known as Deacon's Hill. The couple raised twelve children at the hilltop home, though not all in this cottage. A bigger house was built in front of it in the early 1800s, to which his son A. J. Patterson added a grand Queen Anne-style front in 1871. John Patterson was the first to lay out streets and building lots, erecting homes on some, for a town he called New Paisley after his home in Scotland. An earlier owner of the property, Governor Walter Patterson of St. John Island (Prince Edward Island), planned to found a community called Coleraine until he lost the land to his debtors. There are now both a Coleraine Street and a Patterson Street in Pictou—but no Paisley. John Patterson was not related to Gov. Patterson, nor to Squire Robert Patterson, a *Betsey* settler.

Chapter 3

Churches, Schools, and Hospitals

FIRST CHURCH, 1880

Rev. Thomas McCulloch arrived in Pictou in 1803 on his way to Prince Edward Island, but stayed to minister to the Harbour Congregation. He later founded Pictou Academy. The Harbour Congregation erected a church in 1804, and used it until 1848, when this church was built. Due to a split in the church in Scotland, there were three Presbyterian churches in Pictou for a long time. Those who wished to secede from the Church of Scotland followed Dr. McCulloch to the democratic and liberal Prince Street Church. Devotees of the established Church of Scotland worshipped at St. Andrew's Kirk and voted Tory, while the congregation at Knox developed from a later group of secessionists. In 1918, Knox and Prince Street churches merged to form First Presbyterian Church, using the Prince Street building.

THE CLOCK CHURCH, 1890

Organized in 1846 after several Nova Scotia clergy renounced the Church of Scotland, John Knox Free church opened in 1848 on Spring Street, an extension of High Street. Its clock was a highly visible landmark from both town and harbour. The building was refurbished in 1895, and polished oak pews replaced the old ones. The congregation merged with Prince Street Presbyterian in 1918 to form First Church. The building, with the clock removed, was used for meetings and recreational activities until the United Church purchased it in 1937, dedicating it on August 1 of that year. A new United Church was built in 1964, up the hill from the old Knox church. Knox was demolished in 1966, and the site is now part of Pictou United Church's parking lot.

THE KIRK, DESTROYED BY FIRE, 1893

St. Andrews' congregation, founded in 1822, initially worshipped at the old courthouse on Church Street, which later served as Pictou's Town Hall. The congregation built a small wooden church at the intersection of Denoon, Church, and Coleraine streets in 1823. In 1866 the church began construction of an imposing new brick and stone building on the same site, at a cost of thirty-two thousand dollars.

On the night of November 7, 1893, during Rev. Andrew Armit's first year as pastor, it was destroyed by fire despite a heroic effort by the town's fire department. The congregation rebuilt it in 1895, as shown on the right.

THE KIRK, 1896

Churches, Schools, and Hospitals   55

HALIBURTON CEMETERY, 1905 The headstones of Haliburton Cemetery are visible on the far left of this photo taken from the bridge at Barry's Mill. A group of Pictou businessmen, including cemetery company president James Primrose and secretary Daniel Dickson, established the cemetery on July 10, 1860. Burial plots, sixteen feet square, cost five pounds sterling if they were on the east side of the river, and between thirty and fifty shillings on the west side. Anyone with a five-pound lot could vote as a shareholder in the cemetery. The bylaws included a rule that no one executed for a crime was to be buried here.

**STELLA MARIS
ROMAN CATHOLIC
CHURCH, 1912**

In 1823 Pictou Roman Catholics began building a chapel under the direction of Father James Grant, but it burned the following year. St. Patrick's, later known as St. George's, was completed on Chapel Street in 1828. The first priest was an Irishman named Father Boland. Construction of Stella Maris (Star of the Sea), shown here, at William and Denoon streets, was started in 1864 when the congregation outgrew the Chapel Street building. Stella Maris was consecrated in 1865. The glebe house, on Ross Street to the right of the church in this photo, was built the same year. The convent, on the left, was built in 1876. The parish priest at the time was Rev. Ronald MacDonald, later Bishop of Harbour Grace, Newfoundland, and namesake for a Roman Catholic school built behind the church in 1955. Note the gas lighting, installed in the town in 1853, and the fire hydrant, part of a water system installed in 1901.

St. James Anglican Church, 1912

Anglicans in Pictou had been served by visiting clergy from as early as 1775, but the St. James the Apostle Anglican parish was not organized until 1826, when Rev. Charles Elliott settled in the town. Under his direction, the first church building was completed in 1827 and consecrated on August 16, 1829. The church, uphill and across the corner from St. Andrews Kirk, and uphill from Murdock's Pump, was expanded in 1849, and a rectory built in 1869. The congregation outgrew its building, and the cornerstone for a new church was laid in 1879. It was finished in 1881 and consecrated in 1888.

ST. JAMES, STRUCK BY HURRICANE EDNA, 1954

Disaster struck on September 12, 1954, when Hurricane Edna toppled St. James' graceful spire. The parish, under Archdeacon L. R. Bent, replaced it with a shorter tower, at a cost of $7,500.

Churches, Schools, and Hospitals

WATER STREET CHURCH, 1912

The Evangelical Union Church of Scotland opened this church on the west end of Water Street on January 4, 1857. It soon united with the Methodists, who had been evangelizing since 1798 among the coal miners in the upper towns of Stellarton, New Glasgow, and Westville, some twenty miles inland. The Methodists joined with other denominations in 1925, about the time Mr. Gates was minister, to become the United Church of Canada. This then became the United Church building. It burned on July 31, 1936, possibly ignited by a spark from the railway that ran behind the church. The United Church congregation moved to the old Knox building on High Street.

THE CRADLE OF LIBERTY, PICTOU ACADEMY, 1910

Joseph Howe referred to Pictou Academy as a "cradle of liberty" when he visited it in 1830, about eighty years before this photo of the old college was taken. Under the prodding of Rev. Dr. Thomas McCulloch, the Nova Scotia government enacted legislation on March 26, 1816, granting a charter to Pictou Academy to teach students regardless of their denomination. The following year, philosophy, mathematics, logic, Hebrew, Greek, and theology were taught to twenty-three students in a private home until this building was completed in 1818. The Presbyterian church raised one thousand pounds sterling towards its construction, and the government, which preferred to support the Anglican King's College, contributed another five hundred. The Academy, struggling to survive against pro-Anglican bias and conflict within the sponsoring Presbyterian church, closed in 1844 for two years due to lack of funds. It was reorganized in 1865 as a county facility, with a larger government grant. Under Dr. A. H. MacKay, who became the principal in 1873, student enrolment was too high for this building, so twenty thousand dollars were raised to build a new school on the hilltop overlooking the town. The old Academy building became the West End Grammar School, offering grades one to eight until 1930, and was torn down in 1932.

NEW ACADEMY FIRE, 1895

When the second Pictou Academy opened January 9, 1881, it was considered one of the finest in Nova Scotia, which made it eligible for a larger government grant. However, it was struck by lightning on October 26, 1895, and the ensuing fire destroyed the school and damaged many of the artifacts in Dr. McCulloch's natural history museum housed there. Some of the specimens had already been given to naturalist J. J. Audobon during his 1833 visit to Pictou, and insect specimens had been sent to Glasgow University in 1822. The remaining artifacts were displayed in the next Academy building, completed December 26, 1896, and were later moved to the vacant top floor of the YMCA, where they were found in the mid 1900s and discarded. The third Academy continued to serve students of the town and surrounding areas until it burned in 1938. It was double the size of the first building on the site, with four classrooms, a laboratory, and a museum. A principal and four instructors taught a four-year course of study including ancient and modern languages, physics, biology, zoology, and more. A pass from the Academy was a ticket to any of the province's colleges. A fourth school was built on the site in 1940, and continues to serve Pictou students today.

Pictou Academy, rebuilt in 1896

STELLA MARIS CONVENT SCHOOL, 1917

From the 1870s, the Roman Catholic Congregation of Notre Dame had supported a separate convent school, next to Stella Maris church. Roman Catholic boys attended grades one and two at the convent, and then transferred to town schools, while girls stayed at the convent school until grade nine, then attended grade ten at Pictou Academy. The girls also took junior high home economic classes at the town school. The church-run MacDonald School was built in 1955 on Ross Street, behind Stella Maris, and is now operating as the Pictou branch of the county YM-YWCA.

EAST END SCHOOL, 1912

The East End School, also called the High Street School, was built in about 1872 on the block enclosed by High, Faulkland, Palmerston, and Wellington streets. It served primary and intermediate grades until 1930, when Central School was built at the same block, for a cost of sixty-five thousand dollars. Central's name was later changed to Sir J. William Dawson School, and then to Pictou Elementary. Along with Patterson Elementary, built in the 1940s to accommodate children in Victory Heights, Dawson school closed in 2000 when the new Pictou Elementary opened on upper Wellington Street. Dawson school was demolished in 2003.

THE BRICK SCHOOL, 1916

In 1860 James Primrose constructed this brick building between what are now Faulkland and School streets. He sold it the following year to magistrate Henry Narraway for a hundred pounds, who in turn sold it to the town for four hundred pounds, for use as a grammar school. After it stopped being used as a grammar school, the educational system continued to use it for industrial arts (manual training) classes, and the Boy Scouts also met in the building. It was sold in 1936 to Lloyd MacKenzie, who changed the roofline to accommodate an upstairs apartment. Children's initials, at child-height, can still be seen carved in some of the bricks. This is the oldest school building still standing in the town.

BOYS' RESIDENCE, 1919

The Presbyterian Church built Academy Hall on Beaches Road in 1919 to house male students, who came from all over the Atlantic Provinces and the Caribbean to attend Pictou Academy. They attended church every Sunday, filing into the pews with the residence dean, who lived in a large house next to the hall. Students from nearby communities travelled to class by daily trains until high schools were constructed in other parts of the county. This residence later became the Nova Scotia Fisheries Training School, now part of the Nova Scotia Community College system. The dean's house was torn down, and is now the college's parking lot.

LAZARETTO, 1880

The lazaretto, or infectious hospital, was built in 1848, three miles outside of Pictou in Braeshore, with sixty per cent of its cost raised from local taxes. The small building was designed to house sailors from all over the world arriving at the port with diseases like smallpox or typhoid, and to keep them away from townsfolk. Before the sandstone structure was built, sick and dying sailors were housed in tents outside town. There was a stone table in front of this hospital where food would be left to avoid contact with the patients, and a wooden convalescent home was built a hundred yards away. Despite the precautions, a smallpox epidemic broke out in 1852 when the *Tongataboo* put sick passengers ashore at Abercrombie, a few miles up the harbour at the mouth of the East River. Residents found out and the sick people were ordered back to the ship, but one man sneaked away to a sailor's boarding house in Pictou, where he spread the disease. Another smallpox epidemic struck the town in 1885. The lazaretto later became a seaside cottage.

THE HIGH STREET HOSPITAL, 1895

Mariners received health care at the edge of town, but the citizens of Pictou had no hospital of their own until a group of doctors and civic-minded local women decided in 1893 to rent four rooms in Mrs. George Logan's private home on High Street. Public donations, a Ladies Aid, and a glee club raised $223.50 in its first year, which financed the rent of $7 a month. Mrs. Logan was also paid 50¢ a day per patient for board, washing, and nursing attendance. The first patient was Packles MacLeod, who had his leg amputated at the hip. Many baby boys were named after attending physician Dr. John Stewart. He had studied under the renowned Dr. William Osler, and said a prayer before every surgical procedure. The arrangement with Mrs. Logan ended in 1901 when the west wing of the Marine Hospital was pressed into service.

THE DOMINION GOVERNMENT MARINE HOSPITAL, 1900

By 1878, the federal government decided the town needed a special hospital to treat sick mariners, and not just the contagious ones, so the Marine Hospital was built in 1880–81 on Beaches Road, next to today's fisheries training school on land once owned by Charles Irving. He died without a will, and the property passed to his underage daughter and son. When Emily Irving turned twenty-one in 1882, she deeded the property to the Queen for a hospital, which was already built. The brick-and-wood structure had east and west wards in wings on each side of a two-storey caretaker's apartment, with a low verandah facing Beaches Road. In 1901, its west wing was developed as a cottage hospital, a community-based treatment centre staffed by general practitioners and general duty nurses. The hospital wing served thirty-five patients in its first year, including fourteen with typhoid. The cottage hospital was supervised by Ms. Delaney, Ms. Dunn, and then Ms. Schwartz, all sent from Montreal by the Victorian Order of Nurses. Later Ms. Lottie Kayenburg, who married Dr J. J. MacKenzie of Pictou, was appointed superintendent.

THE COTTAGE HOSPITAL, 1912

When health care needs outgrew the wing at the Marine Hospital, a board began in 1903 to draw up plans for Pictou's Cottage Hospital. The board included John MacLeod, David Purves, John Ross, Howard Hamilton, A. C. MacDonald, Charles Tanner, Dr. Smith Anderson, Dr. John MacKenzie, Mrs. James (Annie) Primrose, Mrs. Jane Baillie, Mrs. Edith MacDonald, Miss Amelia Gordon, Miss Agnes Fraser, Mrs. Margaret F. Logan, and Mrs. Archibald MacKenna Jr., with Mr. W. B. Ives as secretary. John Mitchell of River John was paid $5,500 to build the Acadia Street facility, which opened in 1906. Sisters Charlotte, Sophia, and Mary Russell outfitted the operating room, and their bequest continues to support today's Sutherland Harris Memorial Hospital on Haliburton Road.

NURSES' QUARTET, 1910

Unidentified nurses at the cottage hospital pause from their duties for this photo outside the glassed-in verandah. In those days, nurses lived at the hospital, with no time away except for their annual two-week vacations. That meant they were protected from the public, deemed a necessity as most of them were single women, and they were available for duty at all hours. Their tasks included general patient care—bedpans and back rubs—as well as carrying out medical procedures and assisting the doctors. Many of the early Pictou nurses were supplied by the Victorian Order of Nurses and came from Quebec. Lottie Kayenburg was the first superintendent of Pictou Cottage Hospital, followed by Maud MacDonald, Susan Currie, and then Florence Boa. The hospital got its first X-ray machine in 1925. It was torn down in the late 1970s to make room for a private home.

Churches, Schools, and Hospitals

IOOF HOME, 1925

The Independent Order of Odd Fellows bought Edward Mortimer's Stone House in 1918 for use as an orphanage and nursing home, adding the wing on the left and the kitchen wing, which protrudes towards the photographer. Lodge member John Craig of Yarmouth suggested that the organization sponsor an orphanage in Nova Scotia, never dreaming that his family would be the first to benefit. When his sister and her husband died in Newfoundland in 1923, their seven children were the home's first orphans—the very year it opened. Each Odd Fellow paid three dollars so the lodge could buy the fifteen-thousand-dollar property without a mortgage. One of five homes operated by the order in Canada, the home closed on May 21, 1999, and moved into a new facility next door. The building shown is now an inn. Odd Fellows, dedicated to serving those in need and pursuing projects to benefit humanity, was founded in Baltimore, Maryland, in 1819. The order's name is derived from a seventeenth-century notion that those who help others are odd.

THE NEW HOSPITAL, 1935

The cornerstone for Sutherland Memorial Hospital was laid during Pictou's Natal day celebrations on August 31, 1927, at the Beaches Road site of the former Marine hospital. New Glasgow contractors Fraser, Mason, and Fraser completed the sixty-thousand-dollar building in time for its opening the following year. Matron Susan MacQueen, administrator for the next twenty-five years, operated the fourteen-bed hospital's first X-ray machine. Soon after the hospital opened Dr. G. A. Dunn delivered the hospital's first baby, Clara Sutherland Cheverie, named after the hospital. In 1937, Dr. Fraser Young gave the hospital's first blood transfusion, to Walter Ross of Rogers Hill. Overcrowding in 1944 led Wartime Housing Ltd., which supervised the Victory Heights subdivision, to add a wing that increased capacity to thirty-one beds and allowed for a nurses' residence and an infectious disease ward. After the Sutherland Harris Memorial Hospital on Haliburton Road opened in 1966, this building was used as a training centre for severely disabled children, and later as a drug addiction treatment centre. It was vacated with the 1997 opening of a new seventeen-bed detox centre on Elliott Street, and this building was demolished in 1998.

THE FIRST AMBULANCE, 1940

In 1940 the Pictou Kinsmen Club presented two ambulances, the town's first, to the Sutherland Memorial Hospital. Mayor Thomas R. Hooper is in the centre of the photo, while Matron Susan MacQueen is in the doorway at the far right. The Academy boys' residence, now the fisheries training school, is the brick building at the rear. Over the years, the Kinsmen and Kinette clubs also donated an incubator, laundry equipment, mattresses, and furniture to the hospital. Local residents often brought in home-made pickles and jam for the patients, and the Ladies' Auxiliary decorated the dinner trays.

Chapter 4

Transportation

THE BUSY DOCKS, 1900

Two men and a boy watch activity at the InterColonial Railway (ICR) docks, about 1900. Travellers arriving at Halifax in 1867 took the ICR to New Glasgow, where they connected with the branch line to Fishers Grant (Pictou Landing). There, they caught the railway-owned steam ferry to Pictou for transfer to ships bound for Prince Edward Island and Montreal. In 1876 the ICR finished the Truro-to-Rivière du Loup rail line, which connected Nova Scotia to Montreal and other western destinations, so Pictou port was no longer the only route to Upper Canada. In 1887, the ICR established a direct passenger rail service to Pictou, but the ferry connection to Pictou Landing continued until after World War Two. Pictou remained as the railhead for Prince Edward Island until the early 1940s, and for the Magdalen Islands until 1971.

SAILING SHIPS, 1880

Ships roll up their sails at the entrance to Pictou harbour, about 1880. In 1923 Peter Carroll listed ninety ships sailing regularly from the port, their captains, owners, and where they had been built. He listed twenty-seven built in Pictou itself, twenty-one each in New Glasgow and River John, one in Scotland, and the rest in Tatamagouche, Merigomish and Brule. The most common owners' names were Crerar, Kitchin, Carmichael, Primrose, Ives, and Mockler.

The ships carried away timber, coal, tinned lobster, flour, Hamilton's biscuits, animals, hides and bones, grindstones, Trenton glassware, mail, and travellers. They returned with rum, molasses, sugar, raw tobacco, rice, more mail, and immigrants. Sometimes the ships themselves were exported—sailed across the ocean and sold. Carroll had sailed under Capt. Daniel Munro on Carmichael's *County of Pictou* when it was lost on Christmas, 1879, while en route from England to Philadelphia after delivering a load of lumber. A rogue wave hit the ship astern on Christmas Eve, and the crew struggled to keep it afloat until a steamer loaded with sheep and grain rescued them the next day.

WATER STREET TRAFFIC IN WINTER, 1880

Horse-drawn sleighs pass each other on the west end of Water Street, driving on the "wrong" side of the road. It wasn't until April 15, 1923, that the province of Nova Scotia changed the rules of the road. After that, all cars, horses, streetcars, and bicycles were ordered to travel on the right-hand side of the road. The government issued large stickers for auto windshields saying "Keep to the Right," but it took drivers a while to get used to the change. The rule had changed the year before in New Brunswick, and travellers between the two provinces had some near misses while they adjusted. Prior to the advent of automobiles in 1910, several livery stables operated in downtown Pictou. In 1879, Peter Carroll, the policeman's father, advertised "single and double teams furnished on shortest notice" for weddings, "Pic-Nics," and transport to the railway station and hotels. David Geldart, who had a board and livery stable on Twining Street, lost ten horses when his enterprise burned in 1878. David Kitchin ran the horse-drawn stagecoach from Pictou to River John about the time of this photo, and there were three harness makers listed in the 1879 directory.

PICTOU HARBOUR FERRY, THE *MAYFLOWER*, 1886

Travel from Halifax to Montreal in 1875 meant a roundabout route that passed through Pictou. The ICR train would carry the passenger to New Glasgow, to change trains for Pictou Landing. The traveller would board the railway-owned sixty-passenger ferry *Mayflower*, seen here, to cross the harbour to Pictou. There, travellers could connect with ships to Montreal and anywhere else in the world they wished to visit. Alternatively, the traveller could ride the coal company train from New Glasgow to Dunbar Point in Abercrombie, and finish the trip to Pictou by scow. An earlier steam paddle ferry *East Riding* ceased its Pictou-New Glasgow service in 1874, and in 1876 the Halifax-to-Quebec rail line was completed, eliminating the boat trip from Pictou.

First Passenger Train, 1887

The first passenger train arrived in Pictou in 1887 to great fanfare, and to controversy in the federal government. MP Charles Hibbert Tupper had persuaded $300,000 out of the Macdonald government to build the line connecting Pictou to Stellarton, to the chagrin of Guysborough representatives whom, twenty years after New Glasgow and Stellarton had rail service, still didn't have any rail connection. With W. G. Foster as conductor, the first Stellarton-bound train left Pictou at 7 A.M. on November 28, and returned that afternoon. The tall uniformed man at the bottom centre of the photo is Pictou police chief Peter Owen (Peachie) Carroll. The railway station at the left was torn down and a new station built in 1904 further east, on the other side of the Customs House.

MAIL SERVICE, 1890

The first mail delivery from Pictou to Prince Edward Island was carried by birchbark canoe in 1775, by order of the governor. Methods had improved a little by the time of this 1890 photo of winter travel to Pictou Island, in that the boat was bigger. The boats also took passengers, who benefited from a discounted fare if they agreed to get out of the craft and help pull it across the ice pans. Well into the twentieth century, the mail boat to Pictou Island was fitted with sled runners. The boat would be rowed until it hit ice, and then tugged across the surface until it met open water again. The operator would hop back in and continue rowing. In 1933, plans were underway to replace the mail boat with air service, but the dream didn't materialize until 1949–50. A two-seater plane based at Trenton airport flew the mail to Pictou Island, landing on the only road there.

RAILYARD, 1890S

The cove east of the Customs House is giving way to economic progress in this 1890s photograph. In the foreground is a turntable for the roundhouse, while a railway track extends past Battery Hill towards the marine slip, in the upper left. A chimney from one of the Customs House's many fireplaces can be seen on the extreme right. Pictou's first trains arrived in 1887, but the railway station was then on the west side of the Customs House. The cove, half-silted in by tidal action in this photo, was completely filled when the new Victorian-style railway station was built in 1904, and a new roundhouse constructed on the far side of the cove, at the former site of the Primrose mill.

STEAM MEETS SAIL, C.1895

Steam power meets wind power in this 1890s photo of the schooner *Jacobsea* loading at the InterColonial railway dock. Steam-powered ships had been around for several decades by this point, but sailing ships remained in common use until World War One. When ships like the *Royal William* and the *Richard Smith* steamed into Pictou, the whole population turned out to have a look, but by the time of this photo they didn't attract as much attention. Steam locomotives were introduced in Canada first in Pictou County in 1839, when the Samson, John Buddle, and Hercules engines were shipped from Scotland to haul coal from the mines to the wharf. Diesel trains were introduced in Canada in the 1920s, and the railway companies stopped buying new steam locomotives in the 1960s.

ST. OLAF, 1899 Coal-fired, steam-powered ships did not depend on the fickle wind to meet their schedules, but the downside was that bulky machinery took up valuable cargo space. The ready supply of Pictou County coal meant coastal steamers were especially common along the shorter routes of the Northumberland shore. In 1899, the *St. Olaf* plied the route from Pictou to Prince Edward Island, the Magdalen Islands, and Cheticamp. It often encountered ice in its first spring trips, and would have to put into port to wait for the ice to clear. Here the *St. Olaf* is shown docked in Pictou.

TALL SHIPS AND TRAINS, 1900   A forest of masts characterized the loading area at the InterColonial wharf around 1900, as ships carried goods from northern Nova Scotia to other parts of Canada, the United States' eastern seaboard, and to Europe and Asia. Trains are pulled up to the ships to load and unload cargo, and a small steam tug is visible at the right. A little less modern are the horse teams hauling wagons full of logs, at the bottom left. As sail gave way to steam, the horse teams also gave way to truck traffic. Today, large eighteen-wheelers line up at a modern wharf at the same site, to load pulp from the Abercrombie mill onto ocean-going cargo ships.

LOCOMOTIVE CREW, 1901

A train crew, including Mason MacDonald, fourth from the right, stands next to the steam engine at the Pictou rail yard, about 1901. The Canadian Government Railway, written on the side of the locomotive, was also known as the InterColonial Railway. It was formed at Confederation in 1867 to take over the various railways in Nova Scotia and to construct the tracks between Rivière du Loup and Truro, under the supervision of Sir Sanford Fleming. One of the conditions of Confederation was national rail service. The Canadian Government Railway was enlarged in 1915 to include the National Transcontinental Railways; and again in 1918 to assume control of the Grand Trunk, Grand Trunk Pacific, and the Canadian Northern companies under the name Canadian National Railways, or CNR.

BROWN'S POINT STATION, 1905 Mile Bridge, seen here in the background, was completed in 1887 and linked Pictou to New Glasgow by rail. Soon after, Browns Point railway station was constructed. The Short Line, built in 1888–90 and running between Pictou and Oxford through the junction at Brown's Point, operated until 1985. The tracks were removed soon after, but a line still runs from Stellarton to Abercrombie Point and Granton, across the harbour from Brown's Point. The Jitney, a small diesel passenger train that connected Pictou to other Pictou County towns until 1960, made Brown's Point a popular picnic destination for residents of the upriver towns. Brown's Point, named for John Brown who once lived there, is believed to be the first landing place of the *Hector* settlers, and is now the site of a commemorative park. The railway station was torn down about 1958, and Mile Bridge burned in 1993.

THE *STANLEY* STUCK IN THE ICE, 1905

Ferry service between Pictou and Prince Edward Island was necessary to meet a condition of the Island joining Canadian confederation in 1873. The first icebreaker, the metal-plated wooden *Northern Light*, started service in 1876, and was replaced on December 10, 1888, by the Scottish-built *Stanley*. In 1899 she was joined by the slightly larger icebreaker and lighthouse supply ship, the *Minto*, also built in Scotland. On January 15, 1905, the *Stanley* left Georgetown, PEI, for the half-day crossing to Cape Tormentine, New Brunswick, with a load of freight, passengers, and mail. She met a southerly gale that jammed her into a twelve-foot deep ice pack off Sea Cow Head, PEI. While wind and tides drifted the *Stanley* up and down the Northumberland Strait, her regular schedule continued to be advertised, and the *Minto* kept running—until she, too, froze in at Pictou on February 12. Some *Minto* passengers took the train to Cape Tormentine and walked nine miles across the ice to PEI.

THE *MINTO*, 1905

When the *Stanley* drifted to a point twenty miles east of Pictou, the *Minto* struggled out to help her, getting close enough on February 21 to unload forty tonnes of coal to the *Stanley*, breaking the *Minto's* propeller in the process. With both ships marooned in the ice pack, passengers evacuated over the ice to Pictou Island and Pictou. The ships drifted right around Pictou Island, and the *Minto* almost went aground in shallow water off Caribou. Finally, an expedition set out from Charlottetown to fix *Minto's* propeller and dynamite the ice around the *Stanley*. At 8:30 a.m. on March 17, both ships broke free of the ice, and the *Stanley*, also with a damaged propeller, towed the *Minto* to the ice barrier at the Pictou harbour entrance. The next day they broke through the barrier and, after sixty-six days at sea, the *Stanley* finally arrived in port. By April 1, both ships were repaired and back in service. The government sold the *Stanley* for salvage in 1935, and the *Minto* to Russia in 1915.

PICTOU LIGHT, 1905

The Pictou Bar lighthouse was installed in 1834 to mark the sandbar at the harbour entrance. At the time of this photograph, the lighthouse keeper was Capt. William Munro, (no known relation to the photographer Munro) who lived with his wife and four children in the small, vine-covered home next to the light. The site was accessible by land along the sandbar from Pictou Landing, across the harbour from Pictou. The lighthouse burned in 1903 and was rebuilt in 1904 as this fifty-five-foot octagonal tower. Although the station was automated in 1993, it was considered an active aid to navigation in the harbour area until it burned in July, 2004.

ROUNDHOUSE CREW, 1912 The 1912 roundhouse day shift workers at Pictou station were kept busy in the early days of train service to the town, handling several freight and passenger trains a day. Their job was to repair and maintain locomotives in good working order. To avoid a huge network of tracks and trains running in large circles to enter the workshop, the locomotive drove onto a turntable, and sat there while the turntable aligned the locomotive with a service bay in the roundhouse. The locomotive entered the bay and shut down while repairs—sometimes involving re-assembly—were done. Taking a photo break from the heavy work are, back row from the left, foreman Laurier Campbell, Ronald MacIsaac, Bill Cheverie, John L. MacDonald, Billie Emery, John "Ding" MacCarville, and John Gollan. Front, from the left, are Joe MacLean, Lawrence MacNeill, and Duncan MacMaster.

WATER STREET TRAFFIC, 1912

J. H. MacKenzie had the first car in Pictou in 1910, and two years later Dodd Dwyer started selling them. Area farmers asked the province to outlaw the machines because they frightened horses, and Pictou County municipal leaders passed resolutions banning them on Sundays, Tuesdays, Thursdays, and Saturdays. In 1913 a Pictou constable was issued a stopwatch to catch speeding motorists, and a car ferry was planned to Prince Edward Island. That year, forty-two cars were sold in the county, and by 1916 Fergusons operated an automobile repair garage next to their Pictou foundry. In March of 1923 cars were making the fifteen-minute drive along the ice from Trenton to Pictou, and that October Hector MacCallum of Pictou Island shipped an auto across the water on a "gasoline boat." A 1923 advertisement placed by one M. Mahar called "Star cars" the product of experience, and promised a roadster for $675, or a sedan for $1,050.

SS *HOCHELAGA*, 1930

The Austrian Duke who ordered the *Hochelaga* about 1900 didn't like the yacht, so he sold it to an American millionaire. The craft was renamed *Waturis* and sailed back and forth across the Atlantic until the Canadian government bought the ship during World War One for the Duke of Connaught, governor general, and for use as a Sydney-based patrol ship. In 1924 *Waturis* became the *Hochelaga*, a ferry for the route between Pictou and Charlottetown, and continued in service until the Caribou–Wood Islands route opened in 1941. The ship was sold for scrap, but apparently didn't make it to the salvage yard: it was reported carrying Holocaust survivors from the Netherlands and Belgium to Israel following World War Two. The ship finally sank off the coast of Belgium in the late 1940s, with no loss of life.

SS LOVAT, 1930 William Fraser of Pictou ordered the 175-foot steamer *Lovat* built in Scotland in 1924 to carry passengers and freight twice a week between the Magdalen Islands and Pictou, the Quebec islands' railhead. It also offered harbour tours during Pictou's Lobster Carnivals, which started in 1934. The *Lovat* replaced an earlier ship, the *R. W. Henry*. The coal-burning *Lovat* continued on the route for thirty-six years, undergoing ownership change in 1945, when it was sold to Clarke Steamships of Montreal and renamed the *Magdalen*. In 1960 the ship was replaced with the MV *North Gaspe*, and in 1970 the Canadian Department of Transportation took over the service.

ASHAGOLA, 1944 Ferguson Industries' cross-harbour ferry *Ashagola* was a ride to work for employees from Pictou Landing, as well as a mode of travel for weekend outings to the beach at the Pictou bar. The vessel carried three or four cars, beginning its service every spring as early as April 1. The schedule advertised special Sunday trips to allow for beach picnics on the Pictou Landing side of the harbour. Other harbour ferries over the years included the *Alexandria*, which began in 1854, *East Riding*, which started in 1864, *Mayflower*, and *Maple Leaf*, which all ran up the East River to New Glasgow. The *Maple Leaf* eventually beached at Carson's wharf, at the bottom of Coleraine Street, and rotted away. The fore and aft wheelhouses of the *Ashagola* were salvaged in the 1960s and used as playhouses by local families.

Chapter 5

To Arms

PICTOU ARTILLERY, 1860

The Pictou Artillery, under the command of Lt. Col. J. McKinlay, was on hand for the 1860 visit to Pictou by Albert, Prince of Wales (later King Edward VII). In this photo the men are at attention outside the courthouse, accompanied by one of their two working three-pound brass cannons. The Nova Scotia Militia Act of 1841, which tidied up a mish-mash of military legislation dating back to 1747, decreed that every man aged sixteen to fifty had to enroll in the local militia. Doctors, judges, teachers, and the sick were exempt. Black men were ordered to serve in segregated companies, but none existed until one was established in Pictou during World War One. The legislation said each militiaman was issued a musket, bayonet, and ammunition, but he had to provide his own pack and other equipment. There was no dress code unless two-thirds of the regiment's officers agreed to it, and the militia was bound to perform three days' drill a year—or pay a ten-shilling fine.

BATTERY HILL, 1900

Pictou men grabbed their muskets and first mustered, or assembled as a military group, on this knoll when an American privateer landed at Merigomish in 1776. There was no attack and no need to defend the town. Local lore states that a British navy ship placed cannons here to protect the harbour in 1807, taught citizens how to use them, and then sailed away with the ammunition. Following the American War of Independence, there were fears of an invasion by the New York-based Irish nationalist group, the Fenians, so the Royal Engineers supervised the placement of guns here in 1811–12. The government paid a total of $157,900 to those who took part in Fenian Raid drills in Pictou County. By the time of this 1900 photo, the guns on the left were ornamental, and the thirty-two-pounders on the platform were meant for training and firing salutes, although firing practice was held in Halifax. The battery fired its first salute when Napoleon was routed from Paris in 1814, and its last at the outbreak of World War One.

HIGHLAND REGIMENT, 1912

The 78th regiment lined up in full regalia at the railway station when the Duke of Connaught, lower right, visited Pictou in 1912. The 78th was founded in 1871 as the Colchester and Hants Provisional Battalion of Infantry, changing to Highlanders in 1879. In 1910, they were renamed the 78th Pictou Regiment of Highlanders under Lt. Col. D. D. Cameron. In 1912, they were Pictou Highlanders, under the command of Capt. J. Welsford MacDonald who, along with Pte. Warren Jollymore, was selected to attend the 1911 coronation of King George V. Two World War One battalions fought as Seaforth Highlanders, winning battle honours at Ypres and Festubert in 1915, Mount Sorrel and the Somme in 1916, and at Amiens in 1918. In 1946, they were converted to a motor battalion, and in 1954 combined with the 189th and the North Nova Scotia Highlanders to form the 1st Battalion of Nova Scotia Highlanders.

NONE SO RELIABLE, 1915

No. 6 Platoon of the Nova Scotia Rifles Canadian Expeditionary Force, B Company, 106th Battalion, posed for a photo on the ice near Market Wharf in 1915, with Hamiltons water tower behind them and Brown's warehouse on the left. The company motto, None So Reliable, had the same initials as its title. The group includes Pte. H. W. Carson, recipient of the Military Medal and Bar; as well as privates W. R. Conrad, Henry "Hat" Langille, Henry Little, Fred Shea, J. W. Sarson, F. Siurane, J. D. Shultz, H. E. Sceles; G. E. Hemmings, William Davis, and Lance Cpl. A. M. Gilchrist, all of Pictou; Pte. F. Tompkinson of Pictou Landing First Nation; and Pte. J. J. Patton of New Glasgow. The Battalion, authorized in 1915 and headquartered in Truro, was drawn from northern Nova Scotia and Cape Breton. "B" Company, based in Pictou, was made up of Pictou and Antigonish county men. Training that first winter was mainly shovelling snow and marching. They were sent to England in July, 1916, where the 106th was broken up to reinforce other units. Some black men began enlisting in the 106th in 1915, and on July 5, 1916, the No. 2 Construction battalion was formed—Canada's first and only black battalion.

MONUMENT TO NO. 2 CONSTRUCTION BATTALION, 2004

The No. 2 Construction Battalion was headquartered at Brown's warehouse at Pictou's Market Wharf, also the home of the 106th Battalion, which left for Europe in the summer of 1916. Except for the commanding officer, Col. Dan H. Sutherland, all its men were black, and came from all over Canada and the United Sates. The battalion, which included no local men because there was no black population in the town at the time, stayed in Pictou for just three months before it was moved to Truro, and then sent overseas in March, 1917. The unit spent most of its wartime service in the Jura region of France, supplying timber for trench and bridge construction, roads, and rail lines. The unit remained segregated throughout the war, and the men were not supposed to fight at the front. Some fought anyway, and eighteen of them died in action. The unit disbanded on September 15, 1920. In 1993, Parks Canada placed a monument at the rebuilt Market Wharf in Pictou, commemorating the No. 2 Construction Battalion.

INSPECTION, 1923

Governor General Lord Byng inspected the Pictou Highlanders when he visited the town during the July 1923 celebrations marking the 150th anniversary of the landing of the ship *Hector*. He is shown here speaking to World War One veteran Joseph Linthorne of Stellarton. Lord Byng commanded Canadian troops during World War One. The man on the left, with the top hat, is E. M. MacDonald, Pictou's Member of Parliament and the national Defence Minister. The man in the foreground, in the Highlanders' MacKenzie Seaforth tartan, is Capt. Donald Sutherland. The *Hector* celebrations included a massive army encampment at the Norway Point farm, an exercise carried out annually between 1923 and the beginning of World War Two.

VICTORY HEIGHTS, 1943

With the local shipyard churning out ships for the World War Two effort, the influx of workers stressed the town's housing to bursting point. The federal government's solution changed Pictou's landscape forever. Three hundred four-room and six-room pre-fabricated homes were built in New Glasgow and trucked to farmland east of the town, creating a sub-division named Victory Heights, more popularly known as "The Heights." Only shipyard workers and their families were eligible to live there. Following the war some houses, near the top of the photo, were moved to New Glasgow, and the town took over the administration of the remaining 286 buildings. The rents were raised $2.00 to $23.50 and $31.50 per month, in order to pave the streets in the Heights. Fifty cents of the rent was set aside for garbage collection. Maintenance workers like Grant Murray and Machias Cormier received $115 a month to care for the homes, but $15 was kept back until Christmas, when it was paid to them as a bonus. Renting the Heights homes generated more than seven thousand dollars annually for the town coffers. The homes were eventually sold to private owners in 1971.

The War Effort, 1944

A World War Two advertisement for war savings certificates appeared in a 1944 newsletter at the Pictou shipyard. War loans, later called Victory Bonds, were introduced in 1915 to finance Canada's World War One effort. More than 460,000 posters and a million postcards were produced to coax citizens to "do their bit," raising almost $500 million in two weeks in the 1917 campaign. Local entertainers like Pictou clown George "Twitter" Johnston used their own popularity to support the campaign in Pictou during World War Two. Between 1939 and 1945, there were nine Victory Loan campaigns, raising almost $12 billion from individuals and from corporations. In 1946, the government introduced Canada Savings Bonds to take the place of war bonds.

Flying Ace, 1945

Between 1942 and 1945, Pictou's flying ace George Urquhart Hill shot down eleven enemy aircraft, and was credited with probably shooting down three more, and with damaging nine. The Pictou Academy and Mount Allison University graduate postponed medical school to join the air force when war broke out in 1939. As a flight lieutenant with the 458 fighter squadron, his first air battle involved fighting off enemy planes firing at ships rescuing soldiers from the Dieppe raid. He served in Britain, North Africa, and Italy, was promoted to squadron leader, and received the Distinguished Flying Cross with two bars. He went home to Canada briefly, where he received a hero's welcome, but argued his way back to England, where he trained Spitfire fighter plane pilots. Hill's left hand was paralyzed in a car accident, but he persuaded his superior officers that he could fly with one hand. In April 1944 he was shot down over France, and eventually the Germans captured him as he tried to cross into Spain. After spending three months in solitary confinement and the rest of the war in POW camps, surviving on Red Cross packages, he was rescued by advancing Allies. Hill became a doctor in 1950, and practised in Orangeville, Ontario. He died in a 1969 car accident at age fifty-one.

A Horse on V-E Day, May 8, 1945

This flag-bedecked horse, snapped for posterity on Front Street, Pictou, on May 8, 1945, appears to celebrate the German surrender to the Allies the previous day. The poster announces that a parade, followed by free entertainment, would start at the railway station at 3 P.M. to mark the end of fighting in Europe. The day, known as V-E Day, or Victory in Europe Day, was cause for celebration in Pictou. Not counting those who joined up from nearby communities like Caribou or Hardwood Hill, the town had lost twenty-eight men in action. In World War One, Pictou lost fifty-four.

MARSHALLING PARADE, ABOUT 1946

Members of the Pictou Highlanders line up on George Street in front of the old Royal Canadian Legion hall for this undated photo. In the front row, from the right are Vernie O'Brien, Smith Watts, Ed MacArthur, Roy Cheverie, Carson Morrison, an unknown man, Togo Dalton, another unknown man, "Soup" Hemmings, an unknown man, and an O'Brien. The MacNeill house, now the Pictou Advocate newspaper office, is on the left behind the men. George Street remains a popular place to marshal parades because of its central location and its exceptional width, at least twice the width of other streets in Pictou.

Chapter 6

Pictou at Work

THE NEW BISCUIT FACTORY, 1895

George Johnston Hamilton was twenty-one in 1840 when he began baking brown bread and ship's biscuits (hard tack) in a small building at the corner of Water and Coleraine streets. As the business grew to handle the demand from ships using the port, Hamilton hired more and more helpers. In the 1870s the employees, including an unusually large number of women for the time, posing along the Coleraine Street side of the building, which later became a drugstore and is now a beauty salon and spa. G. J. Hamilton retired in 1883, leaving the administration of the factory to his sons. In 1889, Howard and Clarence Hamilton, the sons in "G. J. Hamilton and Sons," expanded the biscuit-making business to an 85,000-square-foot factory on

HAMILTON'S EMPLOYEES, c.1870

Kempt Street, after threatening to move to New Glasgow if the town didn't offer a tax break. The factory, employing more than a hundred workers, was one of the first to use machinery in the baking business. Clarence retired to Red Deer, Alberta, in 1900, and Howard died in 1926. Under Howard's son, Seymore, the business became a limited company in 1927, and introduced fancy biscuits and candy to the line-up. Marven's of Moncton bought the firm in the 1940s, keeping the Hamilton name. The factory was unionized in 1952, and then sold again in 1955 to Ontario-based Westons, who announced its closure in 1958. The province retaliated with a law saying any firm with fifty or more employees had to give three months notice of closure. The factory stayed open and even added an extra shift, but Hamiltons made its last ginger cookies in 1968. The Kempt Street building continued to be used as a warehouse, finally closing in 1975. Local businessmen bought the landmark to renovate as a hotel, but it burned on September 8, 1980. The Pictou RCMP station stands on the spot today.

ROYAL OAK RUINS, 1872

The Royal Oak Hotel once occupied the corner of Coleraine Street, across Water Street from the Hamilton bakery, but it burned in a spectacular 1872 fire. Here, some of the defeated fire fighters examine the ruins. The fire brigade at that time involved two hand engines, the Phoenix and the Volunteer, and a hook and ladder company. Members agreed to fight all fires, but especially those threatening their own homes. During the Royal Oak fire, the Volunteer sat on the wharf at the foot of Coleraine Street and pumped water from the harbour into buckets. The men of the town passed the buckets up the hill to the Royal Oak, and the women passed the empty buckets back down to the shore. Women helped fight most of the early fires, until the St. Lawrence Hotel on Front Street burned in 1882. The town's population had increased by that point, so there were more men available. They shouldered their way into the bucket brigade, and from then on women were no longer included in Pictou's fire-fighting efforts. The telephone office, later a pizza shop, was built on the Royal Oak site.

CHURCH STREET BUSINESSES, 1878

This 1878 photo of Church Street shows the Wing Sang laundry at the corner of Church and John streets, where there was an Esso service station in later years and now a car wash. St. James' spire can be seen over the roof, and Lorrain's hotel is at the very right edge of the photo. The Wing Sang laundry was operated by Asians, but there is no record of the owners in an 1879 directory of Pictou, although a handful of "washerwomen" are listed. Whether this was due to anti-Asian bias on the part of the directory author, or whether the laundry owners had gone by 1879, is unknown. The relatively short Church Street appears to have been the town's garment district in the late 1800s, for the directory lists thirteen "tailoresses" and "dressmakers" there, compared to less than half that in the rest of the town.

THE WALLACE HOTEL, 1887

The decorations on the Wallace Hotel, on the corner of Front and Chapel streets, celebrated the 1887 arrival of Pictou's first passenger train. The old railway station on Depot Street would have been a few hundred yards to the left of this photo. Around 1900, George Wallace bought the Mason's hall next door to the hotel to enlarge his business. The whole thing later became known as the Wetmore building, when it was taken over by the plumbing and heating company of that name. The next building along the street was the MacKenzie drugstore, later McKenna's. A December 4, 1960, fire destroyed the whole block, including doctors' offices, a dentist's office, the hardware, jewellery, and dry goods stores, a restaurant, the adult education and temperance education offices, thirty paintings in a travelling exhibition, and Ferguson Industries' boardroom.

MCLAREN'S AND THE *STANDARD*, 1891
(OPPOSITE)

A horse-drawn hearse pulls up to the *Colonial Standard* newspaper and job printing office, next to George McLaren and Sons' undertaking and furniture business on Water Street. The *Standard*, established in 1858, moved to the defunct *Pictou News*' former location next to McLarens' after its South Market Street office burned in 1890. The printers employed four pressmen and compositors, as well as general labourers, to circulate fourteen hundred newspaper copies a week. By 1916 the *Standard* was gone, and the *Advocate* was the only newspaper in town.

The white notice next to the door announced funerals for McLaren's, established in the 1860s as an embalming, undertaking, furniture- and casket-building enterprise. Agents sold the caskets all over Pictou County. Funerals were big business, as indicated by the many advertisements of the era for "mourning goods." In 1953 the funeral home moved to its current site on Faulkland Street, leaving the furniture business on Water Street until it was sold to the Sobeys in 1961. The McLarens sold the funeral business in 1968, but the new owners kept the name.

Pictou at Work

PICTOU ADVOCATE, 1893

John D. MacDonald, second from the left, produced the first *Pictou Advocate* on December 22, 1893, when he was just twenty years old. He had worked in the printing industry since quitting Pictou Academy in 1887 to work as a printer's devil, or errand boy, at the Eastern Chronicle before it moved to New Glasgow. He worked at a few other papers, and then, at eighteen, bought equipment to run his own job-printing shop at the *Colonial Standard*'s burned-out plant on South Market Street, where he produced the first *Pictou Advocate*. He moved the business to a former dance hall on Water Street, which burned in January, 1900—but the paper never missed an edition. That tradition continued over the next hundred years, despite changing hands several times and enduring another devastating fire in 1996. After MacDonald, the *Advocate* was owned, either singly or in various partnership combinations, by John A. Fisher, George Murray, his widow Nonie Murray, George Cadogan, Piet van Veen, Ted Teiman, Dirk Van Veen, and finally Bruce Murray (George and Nonie Murray's son), who died in 2004. Second from the right is Advocate foreman for forty years, Thomas McCarville. Local artist Andrew McKnight sneaked into the extreme left of the photo.

THE SLIP, 1895 James and John Yorston, in partnership with John Meagher, built a slip track, shown here under construction in 1895, that could be towed into the water and sunk. Ships would slide down the track when they were launched. Most of the square-riggers of the day had to be "coppered"—have copper-based paint on the bottoms to preserve the wood. John MacQuarrie, Alexander MacDonald, and John Mills were divers at the slip. This was in the "valley," east of Battery Hill, where the wartime Crown corporation Foundation Maritime Company built a slip in the 1940s. The Yorstons built a barque, *Orquell*, operated a fishing boat, *Ada Mildred*, and also owned a steamer, *Beatrice*. James Yorston served twelve years as a town councillor, and two mayoral terms, from 1897–1899.

CAMERON'S TIN SHOP, 1899

A century ago, Edwin Cameron ran a tin, plate, and sheet-iron working business on Water Street, selling everything from a bucket to a stove. In a bill made out to Amelia McKinlay, wife of the one-time mayor John McKinlay (1876-77), Cameron charged $2.35 for a sink strainer, egg-timer, tack-puller, sink pipe, strainer nail, asbestos mat, grater, and a sprayer. The bill was made out in December for items bought in the previous April, May, and September, and was paid in full on January 2. Cameron's was typical of the small shops and services that made Pictou self-sufficient. Ship's caulkers and sail-makers, tailors and shoe-makers, milliners and merchants, carpenters and coal-trimmers, bakers and blacksmiths: they were all important to the town's survival and well-being.

CAMERON INVOICE, 1899

114 Historic Pictou

MURDOCK'S PUMP, 1900

Today, Pictou's drinking water is electrically pumped from a series of wells around the town, but a hundred years ago, residents pumped their own. Here, a boy fills a bucket at Clark Murdock's pump, down hill from the Anglican Church. The water from this pump was reputed to have beautifying effects on young women. There was a public tank on Spring (High) Street, the fire brigade's tank on Tank Street, and wells at Elliott Street, St. Andrews Street, and near the brickyard in the west end. Flycatcher's Pump on Denoon Street, at the bottom of Wellington Street, was called after an entomologist who lived nearby. There was also a horse trough at Flycatcher's Pump. The easy-to-pump One-Armed Widow was at the foot of Margaret Street, and the Primrose Pump was on Water Street, across from today's justice building.

THE REVERE HOTEL, 1900

In 1879, Revere House proprietor Charles Rood aimed at commercial travellers when he advertised "strictly moderate" rates, first class stabling, comfort and convenience. By 1905, the Coleraine Street business changed hands and became known as the Revere Hotel. When the it burned in the wee hours of February 7, 1905, there were ten guests staying there. Also present were proprietor Nathaniel Doherty, his wife Nora and young son, Mrs. Doherty's sister, a chef, two office workers, an elderly boarder, and two kitchen girls. Conductor George Crawford sounded his locomotive alarm after smelling smoke when his train rumbled past the hotel at 2:15 A.M. Most of the hotel occupants heard the horn and escaped, except for the boarder, Mrs. Mary MacEachern, whose body was found in the ruins. The kitchen girls had tried unsuccessfully to reach her and were burned in the effort. Guests leaped from the windows into deep snow, with one man throwing out a mattress to land on. The loss prompted the town to agitate for a fire alarm system to call out the brigade. Damage to the hotel was more than thirty thousand dollars, but it was insured for less than twenty thousand.

BARRY'S MILL, 1912

One of the earliest businesses in the Pictou area was Alfred Barry's mill on Haliburton Stream, almost two miles from the town. The seven-acre site included a woodworking factory, feed and grist mill, and lumber and ice sales businesses. Although it was a busy factory site, as shown here, the spot was also a favorite of photographers, who captured the reflections of trees and rowboats in the still waters of the millpond. The MacLean family now owns the property. Alfred Barry's brother and onetime partner, Daniel, was murdered in his bed at his Willow Street, Pictou, home on December 28, 1921. Money was stolen from his wallet and the house set on fire. Daniel, who operated the Pictou gas plant and was involved in the lumbering business before being crippled in a 1919 accident, was found by a visitor the next morning. George Loder of Prince Edward Island was convicted of the crime, and hanged August 31, 1921.

Munro Logo, c.1912

There are no known photos of Pictou photographic artist William M. Munro, but his trademark, shown here, adorned everything from studio portraits to postcards from 1861 to 1947. He was described as of medium height, with a short red beard. He was a devout Methodist, and a bit cranky. In an 1898 letter he scolded an American customer for giving him short notice of a photo he wanted, saying "you are cramping me for time." He had studios on Water Street and Coleraine Street, where he took photos and developed films. Other Pictou photographers included MacKenzie Brothers on Water Street, Albert Wallace, Wheten, MacLellan, and Laura Hurst. On occasion, photographers from Halifax or Amherst were brought in to do studio portraits in Pictou, and Munro returned the favor by travelling to other towns to work.

The Grain Mill, 1912

The Atlantic Milling Company was started at William Smith's farm at West River early in the county's history, and was moved to Pictou around 1900 by the founder's great-grandson and company president, James W. Smith. By 1915 it was reputed to be one of the best-equipped mills east of Montreal, able to mill two hundred barrels of cornmeal and seventy-five barrels of flour a day. The company imported wheat and oats from western Canada, as well as milling grain for local farmers. It added seed-sorting machinery in 1917, giving it the nickname the "birdseed factory." The market fell off in the mid-1900s, and the mill was demolished in the late 1990s. James Smith was Pictou mayor from 1916–18, before retiring to Moncton to travel on behalf of another flour milling company.

LOGAN AND MURDOCK LOBSTER FACTORY, 1916

Mackerel, herring, cod, and salmon were the fish of choice in the early years. Then, in 1873, Pictou's Con Dwyer tried to can a few lobsters, apparently having heard about a canning operation in Maine. Dwyer's lobsters spoiled, and the idea was abandoned until 1879, when a Pugwash man moved his factory to Caribou. His cans, filled with a one-pound tail, also spoiled, and it was the following year before lobsters were canned and shipped from Pictou. By 1916 the Logan and Murdock factory at Caribou, complete with housing for fifty workers, packed eight hundred cases every season, which ran from April to June at that time. Among the other packers that year, Burnham and Morrill produced a million cans of lobsters; Fred Magee's produced seven thousand cases; and Windsor's packed about five thousand cases. In 1927, Maritime Packers Ltd. began shipping live lobsters to Upper Canadian and American markets. Fishermen were paid 7¢ a pound for them in the 1920s, compared to $1.50 in 1971, and about $5.00 in 2004. The introduction of gasoline boat engines greatly increased the catches because fishermen could cover a larger area each day, leading to warnings in 1913 that the resource would soon disappear. Pictou's first Lobster Carnival in 1934 celebrated the catching, canning, and shipping of lobster, a multi-million-dollar industry, with twenty-five lobster-packing plants along the Northumberland shore worth millions to the local economy. The lobster fleet numbered fifteen hundred boats, and provided seasonal employment to about two thousand.

LITTLE CHILD WITH A BIG LOBSTER, c.1915

PICTOU GARAGE, 1930

The Pictou Garage Company was one of A. A. Ferguson's enterprises, and encompassed a cab service and auto repair shop. Here, Pictou's fire brigade poses in front of the Esso gas tanks with its new pumper, about 1930. Pictou's fire department was established under J. A. Gordon in 1830 as little more than a bucket brigade. By 1864 it had two companies, one made up professional men and the other of tradesmen, with hand- or horse-drawn steam engines for pumping water. The companies had joined by 1865 to form the Union Company, and a crew to operate the hook and ladder equipment was formed with the town's incorporation in 1874. The town placed fire hydrants around town in the early 1900s, and by 1916 there were sixty-two men on the fire brigade. A firehouse, built on Church Street in 1920, was replaced in 1972 with a new one on the site of the first Pictou Academy.

PICTOU SHIPYARD, 1935

Malcolm Langille began working with his father in 1906 as a carpenter at Acadia Mine in Westville, but later went to Pictou Iron Foundry, in which W. H. Davies' company had cast its first iron 150 years earlier. Master craftsman Alan A. Ferguson, who bought the foundry in 1906, taught Langille the pattern-making trade, and he stayed there until after World War Two, making wooden patterns for casting iron. In 1910 the premises at the east end of Front Street included the pattern and carpentry shop, a casting shop, machine shop and foundry, smithy, a boiler house with a seventy-foot chimney, and warehouses. In 1940, the Fergusons oversaw wartime ship construction at the shipyard, a job soon taken over by Crown-owned Foundation Maritime Company. To prevent the shipyard being dismantled and carted away after the end of World War Two, Fergusons took over the assets, although they were not eager to operate a shipyard because of the huge investment. In 1953, the business incorporated as Ferguson Industries, combining the Pictou Foundry and Machine Company, Wallace C. Wetmore Ltd., Fullertons Ltd., and the marine railway. The name Ferguson came to be synonymous with shipbuilding and Pictou.

YARD WELDING CREW, 1942

During the war years, the Pictou shipyard hired many women for what had traditionally been men's jobs, including a Mi'kmaw woman who brought her baby with her on her back. When the war ended, returning veterans sought the jobs at the yard, and the women went home. This 1942 welding crew includes several women. In the back row, from the left are unknown, Wisk Vye, unknown, Owen Langille, unknown, Tom Foley, Clary Holmes, Freeman Saunders, John Williams, Ron Cheverie. In the second row, from the left are John A. MacDonald, Earl Baxter, Harold Trethewey, Milton Veniot, unknown, Jim Teed, unknown, Bill Peterson, two unknowns, Alpha Hale, Vera Williams. In the third row are Freeman Purdy, Steve Casey, Dan MacNeil, Jack O'Brien, Frank Karlick, Howard Lafresne, John Coleman, unknown, Babineau, Joe Cormier, unknown, Clark, three unknowns. Front row, from the left: unknown, Murray Langille, Aubrey Johnstone, Dave Fisher, John MacNeil, Clarence Thorne, Dick Stone, Inez Rudolph, two unknowns, Pitts, Ed Welsh, unknown, Joan Pugh.

THE MOUNTIES, 1943

In 1943, the Pictou detachment of the Royal Canadian Mounted Police was based in a small cottage on a hill on West River Road. The house still stands, but the Mounties moved to new premises on High Street in the 1950s, and then to the current location on Caladh Avenue in October, 1998. Standing on the steps of the 1943 detachment are, in the back row from the left, constables Hector Holton, Les McEvoy, and Donald Fitzgerald. In the second row, from the left are constables Freeman Beaton, Alex Taylor, and A. MacDonald. Staff Sgt. "Rocky" Rockwell, front left, was in charge of the detachment, and the unidentified man on the right was an inspector visiting from Halifax. Mounties had to serve for seven years before they were allowed to marry, and many of these men married while posted in Pictou. They didn't carry guns, and were never posted to their home provinces upon graduating from Regina training school.

Chapter 7

Pictou Pleasures

REGATTA, 1900

Boat races were a popular form of entertainment in Pictou around 1900, when this regatta photo was taken near the quarry wharf at the town's east end. Rowing and sailing races, track events, and piping contests were generally held on September 15, the anniversary of *Hector*'s landing and a public holiday in Pictou. Some of the prominent oarsmen of the day were Lauchie Patterson and "Black Jack" MacDonald of Pictou Island, and Frank Carroll and Dal Patterson of Pictou. John Mills' *Valley Girl* and John MacIsaac's *Black Swan* were the sailboats to beat, and Walter Baillie set the standard for piping. Athletes from Prince Edward Island, Halifax, Dartmouth, and even Boston would compete in the quarter-mile foot race, the hammer throw, shot put, and other contests. For the sensation-seekers, Sgt. Major Baillie would demonstrate how to slice a sheep (already dead!) with his sword.

PICTOU ORCHESTRA, 1906

Groups like the Pictou Orchestra offered relaxation and entertainment, but music was serious business, too. James Dawson, father of Sir J. William Dawson, printed the first music published in the province, "The Nova Scotia Songster," in Pictou in February, 1836. The local five-hundred-seat theatre hired musicians for its eight-place orchestra pit. The town boasted a music school affiliated with the Royal Academy of Music in London, and run by St. James organist Professor T. Singleton at his large Haliburton Street home. It graduated fifty pupils, including six-year-old Catherine Singleton, in 1916 the youngest Canadian to pass the primary grade examination. The instructor at Pictou Academy School of Music, which featured two grand pianos and was housed on the top floor of the Academy building, was a graduate of the New England Conservatory. Academy music students wrote the exams from McGill University in Montreal. The music department was lost with the Academy fire of 1938. John Stramberg, who directed two local brass bands, went on to compose for Lillian Russell in New York's Tin Pan Alley, under the name Stromberg. The town also produced Broadway star Christy MacDonald, and several prominent military musicians.

SELLING AT THE EX, C.1910

In a time-honored tradition that continues today, salesmen set up a booth on the top floor of the Pictou Exhibition building, about 1910. Their wares: Victrolas made by the Victor Talking Machine Company between 1906 and 1929. The selling point: the machines looked like ordinary furniture because the formerly large, external sound-producing horns were built into the cabinets. The Exhibition began as a plowing match in West River in 1817, but by 1851 farmers brought their animals into Market Square in Pictou to show them off, and the event moved to its current location in 1891. It always started the day after Labour Day, and for three or four days thousands paid their fifty-cent admission fee to see who had won prize ribbons. Judges rated hundreds of animals ranging from cattle to chickens, and pigs to foxes, as well as cooking, handcrafts, crops, and floral displays. There were square dances, tug of war contests, horse pulls, horse driving competitions, a dining hall, midway rides, circus acts, and famous entertainers like Hank Snow and Will Rogers. In 1935, the Ex held its first Queen contest.

THE STARS, 1915

The Pictou County Sports Hall of Fame has in its archives a hockey stick reported to have been made two hundred years ago in Pictou Landing, proving Pictou's long connection to the sport. Before the construction in 1937 of the indoor rink on Water Street, an early Pictou team, the 1915 Stars, played in the old open air rink at the corner of Martha and Faulkland streets, across from today's Shiretown Dental Clinic. The team included T. Veniot, Brindy McKnight, Jim Henderson, Lawrence Sarson, Collie Godfrey, Tim Corbin, Frank McGuire, Bernie MacKay, and goalie Clary Henderson. In those days, there was usually just one organized adult team playing at a time, sponsored by various businesses. There were also school teams and pick-up games on the harbour and the ponds.

THE OLD RINK UNDER CONSTRUCTION, 1937

When the new rink opened, watching the Pictou Maripacs play in the APC (Antigonish-Pictou-Colchester) League was almost as exciting as playing. Before ice-making equipment was installed in the late 1950s, the incoming tide would heave, crack, or flood the ice surface, limiting practice time for would-be NHLers. The rink was torn down in the 1970s with the opening of the Hector Arena at the Exhibition Grounds, at the upper end of Prince and Patterson streets. The deCoste Entertainment Centre was built on this site in 1982.

THE LINKS, 1920S

The Pictou golf course clubhouse was the scene of a garden party in the 1920s. The Pictou golf club incorporated in 1921, leasing the former Fogo property from the Pictou Academy Educational Foundation. The club built a nine-hole, twenty-four-hundred-yard course beside the sea on a challenging hillside, but forbade teeing off on Sundays because it was viewed as sinful. The clubhouse is the original home of Judge James Fogo, built in 1854 on the ruins of merchant Hugh Denoon's home, which burned in 1846. The property was known as Belleville Farm, and the Fogo sons ran a tannery and quarry at the eastern edge of the property. The site, with its commanding view of the town and harbour, was used as a signalling station during World War Two. The Pictou Lions Club took over the golf course in 1955, bought the entire facility in 1963, and continues to operate it today.

CHRISTMAS BY THE SEA, 1920S

In an event the town revived in the 1990s, a crowd gathers around a downtown Christmas tree in the 1920s. Instead of Market Square, where today's "lighting-up" ceremony takes place, this tree is at the bottom of George Street. The bottom of the post office railing is just visible on the right, and one can look right up George and Constitution streets to Deacon's Hill. Not everyone had Christmas trees in their homes, but those who did made their own decorations from popcorn, berries, and paper. Some trees were decorated with real candles—with a bucket of water handy! Instead of gifts under a tree or in a stocking, some children just found a collection of nuts, an orange, a piece of barley candy, and a small toy on their chairs at breakfast. Sometimes they would get one item of clothing made by their mothers.

HECTOR CELEBRATIONS, 1923

THE PICTOU HIGHLANDERS PIPE BAND, 1923

Pictou went all out in July, 1923, to commemorate the 150th anniversary of the Ship *Hector*'s arrival on September 15, 1773. The slope in front of the Tobin home, across Front Street from the railway station, welcomed thousands of visitors, including Governor General Lord Byng, who inspected the troops gathered at Norway Point and unveiled the new *Hector* monument. New Glasgow businessman Ray Rogers brought his carnival to the celebrations, airplanes offered rides, and there were parades with the Pictou Highlanders pipe band, concerts and banquets. The town's bagpiping tradition continues today with the Heatherbells Girls Pipes and Drums, an all-girl band that takes part in most Pictou celebrations as well as travelling across North America.

PICTOU TO PANAMA, 1923

In 1923 Jimmie Campbell of Pictou and Capt. Tom Scott of Canso decided to sail their sixteen-foot sloop-rigged craft from Pictou to Panama. By September they made it as far as the Delaware River, where the boat was damaged when it struck a submerged obstruction. A third man, James Maloney, started with them, but quit in Maine, where another man, J. Day, joined the voyage. By the time they reached Boston, the men had regaled American reporters with a variety of stories. They said they were the sole survivors out of seven such ships racing towards Panama for prizes of various sums of money. Another story was that the boat had capsized and they had spent thirteen hours in the water. They also told reporters that the boat was the smallest to ever sail from Canadian waters. This photo was taken before the would-be world travellers left, on the East River at New Glasgow, with the George Street Bridge and the tram bridge in the background. The crew sold the damaged boat in Delaware and returned home, after wiring Pictou for money for tickets.

First Lobster Fisherman's Carnival, 1934

The program for Pictou's first Lobster Carnival promised an event-packed day. It began with a lobster trap competition, and went through tug-o'-war contests, a formal opening event, boat races, beach attraction, concerts by the 78th regimental band, baby and doll carriage parades, bicycle and foot races, lots of prizes, a big street parade, a broadcast by the Dixie Minstrels from MacKenzie's roof garden, a street dance, and fireworks. The July 11, 1934, one-day carnival was the brainchild of Maritime Packers owner William Broidy, who wanted to recognize the lobster fishery's contribution to the local economy and give the fishermen a chance to celebrate the end of the annual season.

CRUISING CRUSTACEAN, 1934

The event was immortalized in a postcard of a giant lobster cruising along Water Street towards Coleraine Street. Today's Lobster Carnivals last almost a week, but they are still held the weekend after the season closes, and they still feature plenty of lobsters, lobster-trap building, boat races, parades, and music.

Conclusion

In the past 220 years, a lot of Pictou has changed—and some things haven't changed at all.

Pictou is no longer a frontier hamlet; lumber barons no longer slide logs down Deacon's Hill to the harbour; Gaelic is no longer the mother tongue; and ships no longer dock three or four deep along the wharves. The old market is gone, and so are the railway tracks, the biscuit factory, and the harbour ferry.

But Pictou Academy still stands on the hill; politics are still discussed with animation and heat; the Scottish influence remains strong; and the harbour will be there for aeons.

The historian Patterson, who mourned the out-migration of young people in 1877, might overhear a similar complaint in Pictou coffee shops today. Peachie Carroll, who complained in his 1923 memoir about the destruction of historic buildings, might be pleasantly surprised to see how many survived to 2004. And John Pagan, or Deacon John Patterson, would be astounded to wander to the Pictou docks today, to see the ship *Hector*—or a near approximation—rocking on the waves.

Pictou's history and its harbour have become the basis for the town's growing tourist industry, with the preservation of historic buildings, annual re-enactments of the *Hector* settlers' arrival and the construction of the full-size *Hector* replica. Pictou's past has become its future.

Bibliography

Barnwell, Annie. "The History of Hospitals in Pictou," speech commemorating opening of Sutherland Harris Memorial Hospital, Wed, June 1, 1966.

Byers, Mary, and Margaret McBurney. *Atlantic Hearth: Early Homes and Families of Nova Scotia.* Toronto: University of Toronto Press, 1994.

Cameron, James M. *Pictonians in Arms: a Military History of Pictou County, Nova Scotia.* Published by the author (through arrangement with the University of New Brunswick, Fredericton, NB), New Glasgow, 1969.

Cameron, James M. *About Pictonians.* Hantsport: Lancelot Press, 1979.

Cameron, James M. *Still More about Pictonians.* Hantsport: Lancelot Press, 1985.

Cameron, James M. *Yesteryears in Pictou County.* Pictou County Historical Society, printed by The Casket, Antigonish, NS, 1994.

Carroll, Peter Owen. *The Life and Adventures of Peter Owen Carroll.* Published by the author, Pictou, 1923.

Forbes, E.R. *Booze: A Reader for History 1305, The History of Prohibition and Rum-Running in Canada.* Fredericton: University of New Brunswick.

Hoegg-Ryan, Judith. *The Birthplace of New Scotland.* Halifax: Formac Publishing, Halifax, 1995.

Jenson, L.B. *Wood and Stone.* Halifax: Petheric Press, 1972.

Macdonald, Clyde. *Notable Pictonians.* Published by author, Pictou, 2003.

MacKay, Donald. *Scotland Farewell: The People of the Hector.* Toronto: Natural Heritage/Natural History Inc., 1996.

McLaren, George. *The Pictou Book.* New Glasgow: Hector Publishing Co., 1954.

Patterson. Rev. George, D.D. *A History of the County of Pictou Nova Scotia.* Montreal: Dawson Brothers, 1877

Sherwood, Roland. *Pictou's Past.* Hantsport: Lancelot Press, 1988.

Shiretown Nursing Home and McCulloch School. *A Different Era* Published by the authors, Pictou, 1999

Teare, Robert. *Teare's Directory of Pictou and New Glasgow.* Published by author, Pictou, 1879.

Photo Credits

Key on page xiii by Lawrence LeBlanc.

Photos are from the Pictou Historic Photograph Society, and from the personal collections of Don MacIsaac, Lawrence LeBlanc, Raymond Gregory, Dolly Battist, Alfred Dalton, Henry Snow, Gertrude Holton, and the author. The photograph on page 16 is from the Jack Woolner Collection, Nova Scotia Archives and Records Management. Don MacIsaac took the photographs on pages 27, 59, 62, 94, and 103.